Lyssa Ro

THE
GOLDEN
LAKE

Wisdom from the Stars
for Life on Earth

from the author of the classic book
The Prism of Lyra

Praise for *The Golden Lake*

[Lyssa's] work is always thought provoking. Reading her books is invariably a delightful treat, and I find myself re-reading most of them over time, finding new gems with each pass. One does not have to believe in channeling or extraterrestrials to gain valuable insight from her work. The content stands on its own.

— Courtney Brown, PhD, Director of the Farsight Institute
and author of *Remote Viewing: The Science and Theory of Nonphysical Perception*
and *Cosmic Voyage: A Scientific Discover of Extraterrestrials Visiting Earth*

Lyssa's unique ability to access detailed galactic history with such loving focus on evolution brings a deep sense of cosmic family, bridging the vastness of space and time into the human experience. *The Golden Lake* offers a profound guide map for humanity's healing and ascension. Lyssa's powerful work continues to be a resource for those that feel a longing for improving life and expanding the power of love on Earth.

— Jamye Price, author of *Opening to Light Language*
and the *Cosmic Consciousness Ascension Deck* (JamyePrice.com)

A new myth is starting to emerge from our collective unconscious, and Lyssa's work is the keystone of that myth. This book helps us to navigate our inner worlds and the outer chaos of our perceptions while using the archetypes of our galactic history that are relatable even to those of us who do not take interest in extraterrestrial intelligence or spiritual principles. It is applicable in our day-to-day lives and offers us a broader, deeper understanding of our reality. I believe it should be a part of every curriculum.

— Vashta Narada (Aleksandra Aleksandrov), intuitive galactic artist (Vashta.com),
seen in the *Interview with E.D.* (Extradimensionals) series on Gaia TV

This profound material channeled by Lyssa Royal-Holt encourages humanity to choose to go through the process of awakening instead of allowing self-destruction. It describes awakening to who we truly are and how to move through our awakening. This insightful perspective helps us to deal with the serious challenges that face us individually and collectively, and it emphasizes the urgent need to do so. As a psychotherapist, I appreciate the deep insights and understanding of how we humans psychologically function and how we can do deep inner healing and become more enlightened to "be in the world but not of it." [This book] is truly a significant offering to humanity.

— Barbara Lamb, MS, MFT, CHT, psychotherapist, international speaker,
and author of many books, including *Meet the Hybrids*

For several years, I have been interviewing channels and the beings they channel for my series *Interview with E.D.* (Extradimensionals) seen on Gaia TV. Lyssa has been on the show twice, and we have more episodes planned. The material she brings through is some of the most comprehensive and palatable, particularly in regard to our galactic history. Lyssa and the entourage of cosmic teachers she brings through seem to have a grasp on our galactic history like no others. They create a framework that is easily identifiable and translatable to our current limited language paradigm. The more we know about our cosmic history and family the more we know about ourselves. This is what our journey here is all about — self-exploration and evolution!

— Reuben Langdon, actor as well as filmmaker of the *Citizen Hearing on Disclosure*
and the *Interview with E.D.* (Extradimensionals) series seen on Gaia TV

Lyssa Royal-Holt

THE GOLDEN LAKE

Wisdom from the Stars for Life on Earth

Light Technology PUBLISHING

For information about special discounts for bulk purchases, please contact Light Technology Publishing Special Sales at 1-800-450-0985 or publishing@LightTechnology.com.

Cover & book design: Gean Shanks

ISBN-13: 978-1-62233-070-6
ebook ISBN: 978-1-62233-804-7

Light Technology Publishing, LLC
Phone: 1-800-450-0985
1-928-526-1345
Fax: 928-714-1132
PO Box 3540
Flagstaff, AZ 86003
LightTechnology.com

This book is dedicated to my students in the United States, Japan, and around the world. Because of your inquisitive minds and sincere hearts, you are responsible for bringing forth this information through your questions and your enthusiastic support. It is because of you that I continue this work.

I am infinitely grateful.

Contents

Preface

LYSSA ROYAL-HOLT

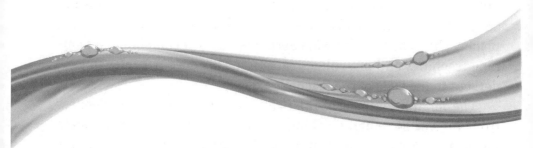

The year of publication of this book, 2019, marks the thirtieth anniversary of the first edition of our classic book, *The Prism of Lyra*, published in 1989. That book was the first of its kind to explore human galactic heritage and the evolution of our star family from a galactic perspective. The groundbreaking *Galactic Heritage Cards*, first published in English in 2013, gives seekers a tool to delve more deeply into their personal star heritage, using the material explored in *The Prism of Lyra*.

As I channeled the material for the *Galactic Heritage Cards*, one thing became very clear: Our star family went through evolutionary challenges similar to what we face on Earth today. All species have a signature challenge, and the healing of that unique challenge shaped who they became as they evolved. Through channeling, and in some cases direct contact, our Galactic Family are now sharing even deeper information about their past roads to healing. These lessons are profound and infinitely valuable to help us on Earth as we face the challenges that await our species. Being on the brink of either self-destruction or awakening, we can use all the help we can accept.

This book is a compilation of some of the deepest channeled material that has come through to my groups in the United States and Japan in the past few years. All of it is designed to help us navigate the challenges we face by presenting a road map to move through this intense process. Many tools are presented here for readers who wish to delve deeply into their consciousnesses and actively work with the inner healing and awakening process. Readers will also learn a great deal about galactic history.

This book introduces the School of the Nine Serpents, an ancient mystery school that originated in our Vegan lineage. The teachings of this school have been given on many planets throughout time and adapted by extraterrestrial mentors in appropriate ways for each planet. The School of the Nine Serpents has two components: feminine teachings and masculine teachings. This does not refer to gender, but to the style of the teachings.

The feminine aspect of the School of the Nine Serpents comes from ancient Pleiadian teachings given by Sasha. Sasha is a female Pleiadian who has been channeling through me since 1988 and has transmitted material for many of our previous books. This material includes the Golden Lake teachings discussed in this book. As you become familiar with these teachings, you will understand why they are part of a feminine heritage of teaching and why feminine energy is of utmost importance in this phase of human evolution.

Feminine teachings must also be balanced by masculine teachings. The masculine teachings of the School of the Nine Serpents are primarily given by the Sirian ambassador Hamón, who began communicating through me in 2013. These teachings are masculine in nature because they give us tools we can actively work with as we navigate our healing and awakening process. The result of using these tools is profound mental and emotional transformation. As you will see, these tools are for the purpose of facilitating inner integration. The Sirian teachings are particularly intense, for in order to transform and awaken their species, they had to do very deep inner work.

Your Personal Healing and Awakening

As in our previous books, Germane — a multidimensional group consciousness system — provides material relating to our galactic history. Germane shares information specifically about the planet Mars and its pivotal role in our solar system. This information was transmitted by Germane as a way to offer a broader perspective on the evolution of our galactic family.

The first four chapters were originally dictated by Sasha for a book published in Japan titled *Ohgon no Shizuku* (*One Golden Drop*). The insightful questions in those four chapters were asked by the president of the Japanese company for whom I've worked since 1990. The remaining chapters are excerpted from channeled sessions and retreats during which the School of the Nine Serpents and the Golden Lake teachings were explored in depth. My sense is that these teachings are just the tip of a very large iceberg. Much more will be coming in the future.

For now, I hope you will use this powerful information for your growth, as I have. The tools have been invaluable in helping me navigate what can seem a very shaky world these days. As we do this inner work, we ignite the light within us and learn how to navigate the unfamiliar terrain that was once unseen to us. This, in turn, helps others along the road.

Gaining confidence about the future can come from understanding our personal pasts as well as the pasts of our celestial ancestors. It is my sincere wish that these transmissions assist you on your unique road of healing and awakening.

For more information and audio downloads, visit LyssaRoyal.net.

✸ PART ONE ✸
BEGINNING THE JOURNEY

ONE

The Lyran Path to Awakening

SASHA

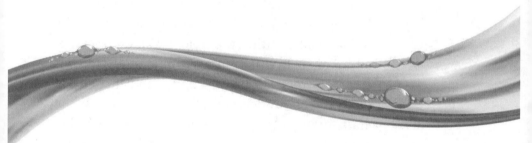

Welcome, readers. Over several decades now, we have presented information about your galactic family through workshops, video and audio recordings, and most notably the book *The Prism of Lyra* and the *Galactic Heritage Cards*. We have found that profound understanding very often comes through your questions, which inspire us to go deeper to provide you with material to assist you on Earth.

Much of *The Golden Lake* began as a book project in Japan, and we have added information from workshops to enhance what we channeled in Tokyo. This book contains images from the *Galactic Heritage Cards* and graphics here and there to aid your understanding. What we share represents some of the deepest teachings we have offered thus far on your world. Through lectures, exercises, and answers to your questions, we will take you on a journey into yourselves and into the very essence of consciousness. Buckle up!

Expression of Masculine Energy

We are honored to be here today and happy to serve. Where would you like to begin?

Let's begin by exploring the archetypal energies of the main star systems connected to Earth. Would you please discuss the main star archetypes and the "upside" and "downside" of their energies, especially how they relate to life on Earth?

Let us begin in the most ancient times with the Lyran archetype. But before we do, we need to give you a starting point to help you see the bigger picture. Because we will share so much information with you, please know that we often use metaphors to describe complex concepts humans often struggle with.

The starting point must always be the One consciousness you all are. Think of it like a golden lake that permeates all creation. In fact, the Golden Lake is creation itself. Everything comes from the Golden Lake. Within the Golden Lake, a fragmentation of sorts began to happen, and archetypes emerged. Your star family, and even you, demonstrate these archetypes. They represent all the main themes the consciousness of the Golden Lake needed to explore. Once this fragmentation happened, polarity was born. The Golden Lake could then experience the paradoxical states of Oneness and fragmentation simultaneously. This is the nature of human consciousness as well.

For the Lake to experience fragmentation, it had to display certain characteristics to help it exist within this separated state. The act of fragmentation is masculine, and thus the first archetype reflects that masculine energy. This is the archetype of Lyra.

The masculine archetype of early Lyrans needed certain qualities to survive and grow the species. In that way, these masculine traits could be considered an upside. For instance, one of the strongest Lyran archetypal qualities is fearlessness and the strength to explore the unknown. You can say they were very solar plexus driven because of that strong will. But, of course, a strong will also has a downside.

If you look at the archetypal qualities of the warrior — such as courageousness, fearlessness, a great sense of duty, and an almost blind focus on moving forward — you can see the downside. Lyrans were plagued by the arrogance and pushiness inherent in a young species. Thus, in order to evolve as a species, they had to marry their strong masculine energy with temperance. That was their biggest challenge in their awakening process.

If you look at humans now, you have a strong connection to that Lyran archetype. Throughout history, you have wonderful stories of noble warriors and pioneers who go into the wilderness and do great things. Those are Lyran strengths. Looking at how the Lyran species matured and had to learn temperance and cool down their hot egos, so to speak, shows an area where humanity needs to grow as well.

Is it true that Lyran temperaments are different and that the Lyran evolutionary process was similar to the human one? What did they need to achieve their evolution?

Yes, there were many Lyran temperaments, especially because the early Lyran civilization spread far and wide into areas known in your mythology as Polaris, Ursa Major, Cygnus, and other constellations. The Lyran evolutionary process is indeed similar to yours. They needed to learn to create balance between their inner male and female energies. Of course, we do not mean gender; we mean the balance between doing (oriented with the solar plexus and the compulsion to push in order to create) and being (an expression of the feminine and related to relaxing, letting go, and moving with universal flow).

They got to the point in their development — similar to where humans are now — where they discovered they could not push any more. Pushing became painful and self-sabotaging, and they began to see that. For instance, people on Earth try to manifest their reality, but they make the effort in a masculine way, and they just get frustrated. One of the biggest changes the Lyrans had to embrace, which felt very counterintuitive to them, was to let go and let male and female energies marry within them. Humans are experiencing this same crucial shift.

It took the Lyrans a very long time to evolve, because they didn't have other species to serve as a reflection. They had to get to a point of much pain, which forced them to look inside. When humans are in a lot of pain, you do anything to commit to change, but you often go back to old ways when the pain passes. Once the Lyrans got to that point of unending pain, they knew it was a signal that the species needed to shift. Their key was looking within, using intense processes of self-observation.

Physically, did the Lyrans have gender? If so, was the dynamic like relationships in Japan, where the husband is usually arrogant and very outgoing and the wife balances that energy?

Your physical bodies are modeled after theirs, but some Lyran species you would have called giants. They were generally larger than humans. Regarding gender differences, because they were so heavily focused in masculine energy, especially in very early eras, men tended to be physically stronger, and gender roles were very divided. Later in their development, women were also fierce and strong. That is part of your archetypal memory.

The Lyran Path to Awakening

For humans, would what be some tips for effective self-observation?

67
Self-Observance

Lyra
FUTURE

A really important key for humanity right now is to observe the emotional body. This is because most humans push down emotions, a tendency that comes from other members of your galactic family. Humans experience emotional pressure in the unconscious from all the repressed emotions you have pushed down for generations. The unconscious continues to repress these emotions as a protection mechanism from emotional pain.

But that emotional energy has to come out somehow, and it very often does so as disease or mental illness. If we were to say what the most important thing is for humans right now, it is to start reconnecting your severed ties to the emotional body and learn to experience emotions in a fluid way. This is necessary to move to the next step of human evolution.

Self-observation means watching — from a place of nonjudgment and allowance — your behavior patterns, thoughts, and emotions that arise on a daily basis. Seeing and owning your destructive behavior patterns is the first step toward freeing yourself from the obstacles that sabotage your happiness and peace of mind. You begin to see where your compulsion to judge others originates: You see traits in others that you fear in yourself. After observation, it becomes easier to make new choices in life. Self-observation also leads to self-forgiveness, an essential part of the equation.

How do you learn to do this deep inner work? We have created a navigational map of sorts to help with this process. The map begins with your original state — the Golden Lake of Oneness. The part of you that separated from the Lake (the golden drop) is a component we call an anchor that keeps you focused here in separated reality. You call this anchor the ego. The ego has a neutral function that is meant, in a sense, to pull you out of the Lake and ground you here to have a human experience. The ego's original job was to be a processor of human experience for the Golden Lake (the One), but its role later became primarily one of protection. When you are separate and have a painful experience in third density, it is the ego's job to protect you from feeling that. Sometimes the ego takes its job too seriously.

Following is a map we created [Sasha's Pyramid Layer's of Experience] to help you navigate out of suffering and back into a neutral state of emotional experience. This was the first navigational map your Lyran ancestors used to awaken. Please follow along as we examine it from the top down.

The capstone of the pyramid is labeled True Self and refers to the state of Oneness, or the Golden Lake. There is no duality or conflict. There is no movement. Everything is balanced and at rest. This is your natural, original state of consciousness. When fragmentation starts, you begin to experience Raw Stimulation. That is the first layer under True Self. You experience stimulation that is inherently neutral. Even though duality has started, it is still neutral energy.

From raw experience arises Raw Emotion, the next layer of the pyramid. You see a sunset, for example, which is the stimulus. The sunset is neither good nor bad, but its beauty triggers an emotional response. The response is often a mixture of appreciation, love, and gratitude. But the response is still neutral, because no story is attached. You do not look at the sky and think, "Man is polluting the sky!" You are simply in the emotion and the moment of the beauty of the sunset.

Those two layers are your natural states before the egoic anchor begins reinforcing polarity. What we call an ego gate is where the ego begins to separate its experiences into preferences. At this point, the stories start. We label this the Ego Filter on the diagram because it creates preferences, such as: "I don't like clouds. I only like orange sunsets in clear skies." Categorization comes in: "Pink sunsets are different from orange sunsets." This is followed by judgment: "Pink sunsets are bad because they're caused by chemtrails." That is how the ego filters reality. You are no longer at peace.

Following the Ego Filter comes the building of Belief Systems, the next level. The ego generates really creative belief systems. Belief

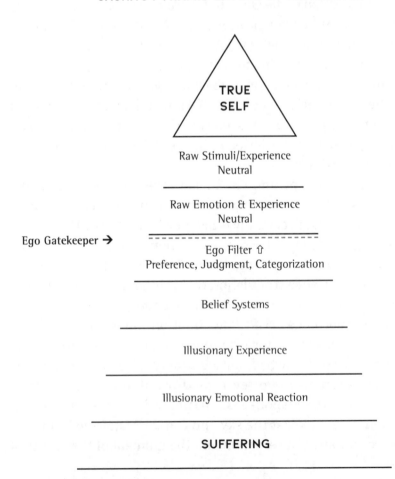

SASHA'S PYRAMID LAYERS OF EXPERIENCE

TRUE
SELF

Raw Stimuli/Experience
Neutral

Raw Emotion & Experience
Neutral

Ego Gatekeeper →

Ego Filter ⇧
Preference, Judgment, Categorization

Belief Systems

Illusionary Experience

Illusionary Emotional Reaction

SUFFERING

systems are interesting, because they can be conscious or unconscious. A conscious belief might be: "Well, I believe I deserve an orange sunset because I did something good this morning." Unconscious belief systems are both stronger and harder to notice, and they often contradict the conscious ones, which can create confusion and suffering.

Belief systems cause further fragmentation. Let's use a human belief system to make the example more tangible. Let's say your father was very abusive when you were young, and you learned that love equals punishment. That belief system goes deep.

The next level of the pyramid is Illusionary Experience, where your belief systems — that love equals punishment, for example — create a state of paranoia. You believe that everyone wants to punish you or push you down, so you walk through life seeing only through the filters that come from your belief systems. Can you see how we're getting further away from the nondual experience of true reality?

From Illusionary Experience we move on the diagram to Illusionary Emotional Reaction. Let's say the person with the abusive father is named Sachiko. I might say to Sachiko, in a neutral or loving way, "That is a lovely sweater you are wearing today." Because of her belief systems, Sachiko hears the comment through her filters and unconsciously hears, "The sweater I am wearing is lovely because the one I wore yesterday was ugly."

You might laugh at the distortion, but this circuitry runs through many people. You can try to give Sachiko love, but if her original programming says love equals punishment, she will never accept love. She will only perceive punishment because that is the only thing she has ever known. You can see how this kind of programming can take you deeper and deeper into illusion, which only results in pain.

The final level is Suffering. Suffering is discussed a lot in Buddhism. Some say, "Life is suffering." In some ways, if you allow this unconscious fragmentation process to perpetuate in your psyche, then life does indeed become suffering. You have the ability to navigate yourself out of the state of suffering. With awareness and self-observation, you can move backward through the layers. It takes practice and a lot of self-honesty to do this.

For example, if Sachiko is suffering, she thinks a lot about my comment about her sweater. Maybe she replays it in her head, or maybe she is not conscious of it but just feels badly and doesn't know why. If she can identify the reason for her suffering, she can navigate backward, see that it is an illusionary emotional reaction, and ask herself where it came from. With further self-inquiry and observation, she can navigate backward again to see where the illusionary feelings came from. She will see that they came from the comment made about her sweater. Then she can keep navigating backward to find out why it bothered her so much.

As you move backward on this pyramid, the Belief Systems layer is the hardest to work through, because the layers are disguised. Many people do a lot of work in this layer in meditation. As we've said, sometimes you have conscious belief systems that are easier to identify. The unconscious ones are harder to identify, because you have to learn to listen to the whispers. They are like little gas bubbles. When you are quiet — like when you meditate or enjoy a sunset — a thought might bubble up that says, "You shouldn't be watching the sunset. You should be working. You don't deserve peace until your work is done." These discoveries are like gold. Cherish them, because they are the keys that unlock you to move backward through the layers. They are the keys to your freedom.

If you move backward through the layers, you eventually move into the Ego Filter level, where feelings are based on preference, judgment, or categorization. Then there is another gate. For some, this gate is the hardest to move through, because in order to move backward through the layers — which leads to a state of nonduality — you have to let go of the ego's addiction to categorize, judge, and prefer. This is an area of intense spiritual training, and many of your galactic ancestors had to do this training on their paths to awakening. In Japan, monks in Zen monasteries train to purge attachment. That training helps them move through this gate.

As many of your ancestors learned, too much spiritual discipline just creates more suffering. So a middle road is important. Attachment isn't really the problem; self-judgment is the problem, because it empowers the anchor. As you become aware of this process and learn to navigate the layers, you will find yourself spending longer periods resting in the state of nonduality. That doesn't mean you walk around like a zombie. (That is one of the stories the ego will tell you in order to keep you in fear of letting go of judgment). Once you get past that egoic gate, you move into a spectrum of reintegration on your way to merging with the Lake once again.

So at the top of the pyramid, we experience neutral emotion? Did the Lyrans have the same emotional experience?

Yes. The experience of neutral emotion, which is a completely different spectrum of experience, is what awaits you as you evolve. It is not an absence of emotion. In fact, it is deep emotion but without the stories attached that lead to suffering. Your Lyran Galactic Family took a long time to awaken, but they eventually followed this navigational map through self-observation. We present it here because this map is familiar to you on a deep level through the experiences of your Lyran Galactic Family. We will talk more about these awakening processes as we move through this book. Now, let's look at your Vegan Galactic Family.

TWO

The Vegan Lineage

SASHA

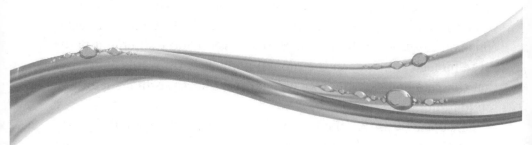

From Lyra, we move to Vega. As you will see, Vegan characteristics actually planted the seeds for the challenges and characteristics of other members of your galactic family. As we mentioned, Lyrans chose to express more of their masculine energy, especially in their early eras. However, groups within the Lyran lineage that didn't really connect with masculine energy and wished to live a different way. They wanted a more spiritual, inwardly focused existence. These groups migrated to star systems in the direction of the star Vega, as seen from Earth. This was the beginning of the Vegan lineage.

At first, these very early Vegans attempted to explore more of the feminine expression, or what they believed was a focus on spirituality. They developed a number of spiritual practices, including meditation, because they wanted to go back Home to the Lake, so to speak. But something very interesting happened that became a detour on their road Home. After generations sought to connect with feminine

energy, they started to split internally, splitting the mind and the heart, or the masculine and the feminine. Instead of a balanced expression of the duality of the universe, they focused on the mind, deluding themselves into thinking it was a true spiritual path. They believed perfection of the mind and eradication of emotions would bring them spiritual perfection. Their beliefs about the role of emotions were flawed, and this split widened over generations.

When we talk about emotions, we include the capacity of the heart to love. If you push down negative emotions, you also push down the heart's capacity to love. This is what happened with the Vegans. They became extremely mentally focused and emotionally dry. The icon you know as Mr. Spock from *Star Trek* is a perfect example of Vegan consciousness. They channeled all the passion and excitement natural to biological beings to the mental body. It is from this condition that the Zeta beings, whom we will address shortly, established their foundation.

The upside was that the Vegans developed an innate ability to connect with natural spirituality, similar to Japanese Shintoism and other indigenous spiritual orientations that revere nature. Throughout the galactic family, there is a spiritual system we call Vegan mysticism that has influenced nearly every group in the galactic family, including Earth. Shintoism is just one of Earth's spiritual systems influenced by Vegan mysticism. Vegans had a tremendous capacity for spiritual connection, but when they began to create the split between heart and mind, the downside revealed itself. This split spread through many other galactic civilizations, all the way to Earth.

You might ask why this happened. There are two aspects of that question we wish to answer. There is the little why (the microcosm) and the big why (the macrocosm). The macrocosmic answer has to do with the Golden Lake and its original intention to experience separation. Fragmentation is a masculine act; therefore, all the journeys of your galactic family are tainted with masculine energy, which leans toward separation. This archetype affects all aspects of creation. The act of separation is masculine, and the act of integration is feminine.

It is hard to connect with the process of integration while still cling-ing to separation.

The little why, or the microcosmic interpretation, is that even though they focused on spirituality — which is inherently male-female balanced — they were still influenced by the big directive from the One. That directive compelled them to experience the masculine energy of separation. This led them to believe that if they could just refine their mental bodies — the source of masculine energy, as they saw it — they could progress more spiritually. The irony is that they still displayed Lyran characteristics but in their inner selves rather than in their society. As time went on, they fooled themselves into thinking they were more spiritual, but they had just re-created the Lyran dynamic in their own way.

Why did the metaphorical Golden Lake want to experience separation?

When you are fully integrated, as the Golden Lake is, there is no move-ment; it is completely still. It is both the beginning point and the end. We Pleiadians believe that the flow of the universe moves like a mobius (or an infinity symbol), much like an in-breath and an out-breath. The universe goes through cycles of separation and integration. Everything is paradoxical because these seemingly opposite states exist simultane-ously, but the human mind can now only perceive one at a time. As you spiritually evolve, you'll be able to perceive your dual nature without experiencing the discomfort of the paradox. It isn't that the Golden Lake wanted to experience separation; it was just part of the cycle.

This separation can be a key for growth. You are still the Lake; you will always be the Lake. This little person in the human body still expresses the Lake. The consciousness that looks through your eyes is the Lake. But because of the anchor of the ego, it mostly thinks it is separate, except for rare moments when you feel that connectedness.

We always see the Golden Lake, so can we go back to it anytime?

Keep in mind that you cannot see the Golden Lake as something outside of you, because you are the Golden Lake. The only thing that stops you is your ego, which is like an anchor weighing you down. The Layers of Experience diagram in the previous chapter is like a road map. It shows you how to navigate your emotions, your belief sys-tems, and your thoughts, to help you return to Lake consciousness.

So the Vegans suppressed their emotions. Since love is an emotion, did they suppressed it too?

Yes, but they didn't believe that's what they were doing. Their love was very mental.

What is the origin of love? Can you define love?

The origin of love is the golden light of the Lake. It is you. You are that Lake. The human concept of love is very different from the true experience of it. You usually believe love is triggered by something outside of you. But love really is your original state. When all obstacles to your original state are removed, only love remains. This is much like how the sun always shines but it is sometimes hidden by clouds. Disowned human emotions, beliefs, and attachments are like those clouds. Remove them and only the sun remains. Thus, love is the primordial energy of the universe. It is not an emotion — only humans label it that way. As your species evolves, you will learn to feel love without any external stimuli. You will learn there is nothing devoid of love. It is the whole universe itself. It is also you.

There are many small and limited definitions of love. Most humans think love is only between partners.

Love between partners (no matter the gender), especially in the state where you are being physically intimate, is a way that you can experience the primordial energy of the universe — if you drop your barriers. This is one reason for the sexual act. Older species, such as Pleiadians and others that have almost finished their incarnational cycles, believe the act of intercourse is not as important, because we feel that love between us at all times. It is more important for humans, because it gives you the opportunity to connect with each other and reconnect with the universe.

How did the Vegans evolve?

At a certain point in their evolution, the Vegans saw the split in themselves. They'd had the split for so long, it was hard for them to shift quickly. Much like the Lyrans, it required self-observation. Actually, self-observation is one of the keys for all older species to facilitate their awakening process, as it will be for you. Because of their many spiritual practices, they had the discipline and motivation to make these shifts, but they did not happen quickly.

By observing themselves honestly, they were able to see the split, and then they had to reaffirm their spiritual commitment in a new way. Remember, they originally thought they were spiritually committed, because they wanted to focus their energy internally. But they ended up splitting within themselves. As a result, they had to return to their emotional bodies and heal themselves from there. They had seen what happened to the Zetas, who were part of their genetic line, and they were determined not to repeat the same pattern.

The Zetas

Within the Vegan lineage, one branch became extremely mentally focused. Their intent was to develop the mind and eradicate emotions, mistakenly believing emotions were a sign of lesser-evolved species. This group created a very large split within themselves. They didn't really understand what they were doing but convinced themselves they were on the path of perfection. This is the civilization we have called the Zeta Reticuli, or the Zetas for short.

As this civilization went through its developmental process, its people had problems. They were not able to procreate easily, and their planet became very toxic. Even their bodies became weaker. However, seeing these symptoms, they still did not recognize the connection between their personal and planetary conditions with the split they had created. They didn't understand that you cannot eradicate emotion. Trying to do so only pushes emotions deeper and creates conditions of toxicity — both internally and externally. Thus, they continued moving forward in their process of "perfection," nearly to the point of extinction. They became so focused on the mind, so limited in their linear thinking, that they could not see the obvious.

Because the Zetas would not admit to the emotions surrounding their crisis, they became desperate. Searching for a solution to their species' problems, they reached out to the Golden Lake through their spiritual practices. The idea of the Lake was somewhat theoretical to them, but because of their desperation, they opened themselves just enough to concede that perhaps there was something more than the reality they had mentally envisioned. In connecting with the Lake, a group consciousness answered — the Founders. These beings play the role of architects of the whole journey of separation and eventual reintegration. The Founders communicated to the Zetas that in order to heal, they needed to reintegrate their emotional bodies. Of course, the Zetas did not want to do that. They really did not understand its importance.

How did this reintegration with the emotional body happen? The Founders brought humans and Zetas together to learn from each other and take the next steps in their evolutions. The Zetas have used some genetic material from humans, who still have emotional bodies, to help them rebuild and physically strengthen their species. More importantly, when a human and a Zeta communicate with each other, there is a tremendous amount of fear. From the point of view of the Zetas, humans are wild creatures and unpredictable. Zetas experience a lot of fear while not really understanding what fear is. When humans encounter Zetas, they too experience fear, because Zetas represent the unknown — the strange "other." These encounters trigger primal fear for both species.

These interactions have been important for humans and Zetas, because they allow both to confront their fears on a collective level. We have spoken about upsides and downsides. If there is an upside to the Zeta experience, it is that they have an innocent passion for their self-evolution even though their passion nearly destroyed their species.

Their innocent passion is very beautiful. However, the downside with the Zetas of this era is that their vision is often constricted. They rely too much on logic, reason, and linear thinking. They cannot see options outside their paradigm. That is why they nearly destroyed their species.

The contact programs between humans and Zetas have been going on for hundreds of years, but it accelerated from the 1940s to the present. This contact has been very important, as you will see.

So the Zetas created a hybrid race with humans to benefit their evolution. In terms of a timeline, didn't the hybridization occur a long time ago?

Explaining this is a challenge, because the Zetas work outside of time. For example, if you have a straight line that represents the human view of time/reality, the Zetas hover over that line. They can go to any place on the timeline. They did experiments thousands of years ago and even more during the 1960s through the 1990s.

Why did it start in the 1940s?

It began at this time, anthropologically speaking, because when a planet achieves nuclear capability, everybody "out there" starts paying attention. So as far as the human timeline, it is very recent. If you look at the parallels, your planet is moving very quickly now toward space travel, so it was necessary.

It is hard to imagine being totally devoid of emotions.

The Zetas were convinced they had eradicated emotions, but when they began their genetic engineering, they eventually discovered they hadn't killed the emotional body. They had just severed their connection to it. The energy field was still there.

What would happen if humans did the same thing?

Most likely you will go down the same road. If you look at probabilities, there is a timeline where that is exactly what humans do. It is not the strongest probability right now, but it is a possibility.

So what kind of dynamics happened to get the Zetas to connect to the Lake and see what was really happening?

We mentioned this earlier regarding the Lyrans. When internal pain reaches a critical mass, the pressure becomes so great that it forces you to look for alternatives, some you might not intellectually embrace. This is one reason for the value of pain in human reality and in the realities of your galactic family. Pain forces you to look outside your familiar paradigm.

Do the Zetas have male and female genders, and do they procreate?

During the time when they experienced their species crisis, they couldn't procreate. Look back at the conversation we had earlier about sex and the importance of opening yourself during the sexual experience to be able to connect with the Lake. The Zetas were so closed that the sexual act became robotic, with no openness. That is one reason they were not able to procreate. Their expression of gender depends on the era of their evolution, but on the genetic level, they have XX or XY chromosomes that don't really affect the physical being in any significant way.

So the mingling with Zeta DNA helped to create a quantum leap on the part of humans?

Yes. From our point of view, it's quite exciting. When contacts first started more frequently in the 1980s and 1990s, humans had a lot of fear. We spoke with many humans at that time about this. We talked to them about the importance of using that contact experience as a way to work with fear. Now, a few decades later, the majority of contacts with Zetas are not fearful. This shows a quantum leap in which humanity has stepped through their fear on a very deep level. It is like an initiation before a species can travel to the stars.

Can you elaborate on using fear to evolve?

This idea is based on the use of polarized energy. Fear and it's opposite, love, form a polarity relationship. You cannot go back into the Lake if you cling to a fearful paradigm; the energies are not compatible. To get to the Lake, you have to pass through the doorway of fear. Returning to the diagram of the Layers of Experience, we mention the ego gate. Fear is one of the metaphorical soldiers standing at that gate. The ego doesn't want you to go back to the Lake, the original state of Oneness. It uses fear as a way to stop you.

Is it a valid methodology to maximize fear in order to merge into the Lake?

That question is very Vegan in style. Yes, it is valid, but it depends on the intention. There is a story of Buddha's enlightenment, where he meditates under the bodhi tree. Before he reaches enlightenment, he experiences his greatest archetypal fears and has to face them, including demons and all the projections of the shadow within. It is almost too much for him to bear. But he stays with the process, walks through the doorway, and is enlightened. This process is organic and cannot be artificially induced until a person is ready.

The Essassani

Since you were talking about fear regarding the relationship between humans and Zetas, would you please talk about the result of that relationship — one of the hybrid races known as the Essassani?

We were talking about the Zetas doing hybrid work with humans. This created many lines of hybrids, some known and some unknown. Some lines were weak and did not survive. Others matured and eventually went off on their own into the universe. The most famous is the civilization of the Essassani.

102
Alchemy

Essassani
PARALLEL

The civilization of the Essassani is extremely important to humanity. It represents a possible future timeline for Earth. Genetically, they are part human and part Zeta. But what they also represent is a type of alchemy. We spoke of fear and love and how a type of alchemy happens and everything is transformed when you allow yourself to pass through the energy of fear. This is why the Essassani species is so awakened. Their birth came from that alchemy of fear and love. This is why, when humans listen to the channelings of Bashar through Darryl Anka, they can feel the power of that alchemy. It gives them confidence that they, too, can walk through their fear.

So the Essassani represent the future of humanity?

Yes. Bashar has said that even though they are a hybrid of humans and Zetas, they also have their ancient history. We know this might be a little confusing for some humans, since we said the 60s, 70s, 80s, and 90s were the peak of this work. So how could the Essassani have an ancient history? The timelines are not parallel. When we said the Zetas hover above the human timeline, they could actually interject that genetic line at any time in the timeline when working with their genetic projects. From a human point of view, the line was inserted in the ancient past to give the Essassani time to develop as a species.

So the upside of the Essassani is that they are an integration of love and fear?

That is one upside. Another upside has to do with their qualities of integrity. This means their thoughts, emotions, actions, and intentions are all in alignment. That is, in a sense, a perfect model for a civilization, because what results is the creation of authentic beings.

If we were to say there is a downside, we notice that from a human point of view, Essassanian solutions to human challenges seem too simplistic for many humans. The execution of the Essassani philosophy in a human reality is difficult for humans, and the depth of their philosophy isn't yet fully understood, no matter how clearly Bashar might communicate it.

The Orions

To talk about the Orions now, we have to go back to Lyra and Vega. As we said, these lineages have many branches. Some of the branches from Lyra and some from Vega joined together and eventually became the Orion civilization. For readers not familiar with the Orions, they represent the most polarized civilization that ever existed in your galactic family. The dynamic was threefold: There was a very controlling empire, much like if you imagine a dictatorship on Earth, but multiplied by a million; there was absolute control. The population being controlled struggled with victim consciousness. Finally, a secret group of resistance fighters called the Black League sought to free the Orion people from the empire. (The word "black" is used to mean "hidden.") The intention of the Black League was positive, but in terms of polarity dynamics, they exacerbated the problem. As long as there are two sides that continually fight, they will always stay locked in the polarized energy of retribution.

For millennia, the Orion civilization was locked in this polarity drama. Their awakening happened in a very intense and unusual way and had to do with the conception and birth of a very special being that you could call an Orion Christ. We mentioned how the Zetas were desperate and called to the metaphorical Lake. The same thing happened to the Orions. In the darkest time, the Orion Black League priests became desperate, and they called out to the Lake. The priests received an answer, which had to do with performing a ritual to conceive a child with a priest and priestess. A symbolic drop from the Lake would incarnate in this special baby, untainted by the polarity perpetuated in Orion for millennia.

The intention was that the energy of pure integration from the Lake would incarnate, and the frequency could start to change the

55
Fusion & Magic

Orion
PRESENT

dynamic in Orion. This is a very unusual way to shift a civilization that really only works with a civilization in intense conflict. But even more deeply than that, it was simply a matter of timing. Energetically, the intense polarity had reached a tipping point, as all polarity eventually does. When they reached out to the Lake, the dynamic was about to shift anyway. The birth of the Orion Christ helped the process along; it was a symbolic way to focus the energy of Orion's transformation.

Regarding upsides and downsides, we would say one upside of the Orions was their intense focus and passion. Orions never saw the emotional body as negative. Except for priests, they expressed their passion in an uncontrolled way, almost to the opposite degree of the Vegans. They were extremely loyal and dedicated to their cause, and they experienced deep love. You can see how this state of being is a combination of both their Lyran and Vegan attributes. The downside was that their passion kept the conflict in place. They did not know how to balance their emotions. They could harness that energy for magical practices at times, but they couldn't see the larger picture.

How did the Orions eventually heal their polarity?

We have found that the best way to describe this is with metaphor. Imagine you have two really powerful magnets, and the direction they are turned causes them to repel each other. When you put those magnets under the pressure of repulsion, it creates a new energy field: compression. Scientifically, you would call it a type of fusion. When you create fusion, it forces together two opposites that create a release of energy. The force of the polarity in Orion, through its massive compression, created an unstable energy field that generated a process of fusion.

The story of the Orion Christ is a literal story, but the story of the magnets is a metaphorical one to illustrate polarity dynamics. Energetically at the point of fusion, when a new energy source is released, it creates a torus field of integration. It was at that moment that the Orion Christ was born. The Orion Christ was the physical representation of this energy-dynamic process. He embodied the energy of fusion, which is complete integration.

It seems like you might die from that kind of pressure.

They nearly did. On Earth, Israel is an example of this kind of pressure, but that is a very weak example compared to Orion. The pressure is extremely hard to bear. The pressure was held on the level of planetary consciousness, not just the consciousness of one person. Because of their level of extreme focus, they could bear more than perhaps a Lyran could.

These types of awakening experiments have also been done on your world, such as with Jesus Christ. It did not work, because human energy dynamics are different. Instead of helping to facilitate a fusion and subsequent integration, your planet instead created a religion in which many people died in Jesus's name — the exact opposite of his intention.

Has the Orion Christ been to Earth?

Think of him as a drop from the Lake. All Christs and Buddhas are drops from the Lake. They come out of the Lake and return to the Lake. You can't even say they are souls, because they don't have an identity as such. They serve a different function. When they incarnate, they are very often misunderstood. Humans attach to them instead of understanding that these Christ drops are meant to remind you that you are also a drop, and that is your true nature.

What makes normal humans different from these Christ/Buddha drops? Is it the size of the drop?

There really is no qualitative or quantitative difference. They are drops from the Lake, as are you. The biggest difference is that the consciousness of the drop incarnates with full understanding and expression of its true nature. This is your potential too because you are as much a drop of this Lake as they are. Since the Lake is still learning about separation and polarity, some aspects of the Lake incarnate with little or no memory, and some aspects incarnate with full memory. From the bigger picture, the whole process, while simple, is perfectly balanced like the most intricate machine. Everything always balances out. In times of deepest polarity, the greatest light emerges from the Lake to remind you of your essence if you are willing to see it. As polarity begins its integration process, the light amplifies within all drops of the Lake. This is what has begun now, and it why so many on your Earth cling to the old paradigm of separation. A change this huge is frightening to many. But there is no stopping this process now.

THREE

Our Diverse Galactic Family

SASHA

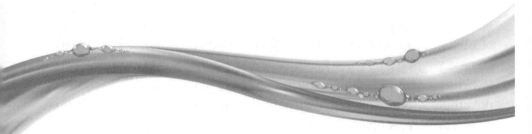

We now move on to the biggest helpers of humanity and some of the energies that have had a profound importance on the awakening of humans on Earth. First, we start with the Pleiades.

The Pleiades

In order to talk about the Pleiades, we have to go back to Lyra, because the Pleiadian Galactic Family came primarily from the Lyran lineage. As mentioned, the Lyrans tended to express themselves in a more masculine way as a civilization. But many civilizations branched out from Lyra, and one group was not really attracted to the masculine expression. They colonized new areas of space in order to form a civilization more in alignment with their preferences. The stars in the sky you call the Pleiades are young stars. The true Pleiadian colonies are in the direction of the Pleiades, but originally were not the stars of the

39
Imbalance in Positive Polarity

Pleiades
PAST

Pleiades themselves. One genetic line moved from the Lyran civilization to that area.

Meanwhile, another branch from Lyra came to Earth in the early days before human beings. This Lyran branch lived on Earth for many generations, mostly in the area you know as Scandinavia and Northern Europe. This group had some trouble adapting to the conditions on Earth, so they took some genetic material from primates and integrated it within their DNA to help their bodies adapt to this planet. They lived happily here for hundreds of years. Eventually, for reasons we shall not discuss here, they chose to leave Earth, and they joined some other groups that had left Lyra and colonized the area of the Pleiades. The Pleiadian civilization was born when the two lines joined. Thus, there are two genetic lineages of Pleiadian people: One is pure Lyran, and the other is Lyran with genetic adaptations from Earth.

The ancient Pleiadian history is probably not as dramatic as some of the others we've discussed, such as Orion. Regarding upsides and downsides, the biggest upside is that the Pleiadian people have a tremendous capacity for love, compassion, sharing, and a deep sensitivity. The downside, which is a very big downside, is that the ancient Pleiadians never wanted to see their shadows. They were very happy to embrace the positive, but they always pushed down the negative. As you can imagine, that created an imbalance. Over time, the Pleiadian civilization became increasingly out of balance. They began to create something similar to what you might call a plague that affected their immune systems. The best healers tried everything and could not find a solution. Just as with other civilizations, the crisis led Pleiadian spiritual leaders to reach out to the Lake. They received information about the meaning of the plague, and it shocked them. They were shown how they had created imbalance through their unwillingness to embrace the shadow.

As a people, the Pleiadians had to experience a lot of deep soul searching and inner work. Eventually, they made the shift, but even now they still tend to focus on the positive. Because of this tendency, the Pleiadian people can sometimes be a bit naive and blindly enthusiastic, especially when they were a younger species. Pleiadians train themselves to consciously integrate both the shadow and the light in order to counteract this inclination.

Do humans have Pleiadian genetics?

Yes, but you are a genetic mix from many of your Galactic Family, which accounts for the wide diversity of body sizes and shapes, skin colors, eye colors, hair textures, and so on. Many of your researchers look for "alien" DNA in genetic samples of possible bodies recovered or unearthed on your world. But since the vast majority of humanoid life in the galactic family comes from an original genetic template, even DNA from extraterrestrials won't seem too alien, because you are related.

Just like the Pleiadians, it seems that through disease, people can become aware of old patterns and grow from them. Can you elaborate on disease and growth?

We were discussing earlier how pushing down emotional energy can create illness. For the great majority of humans — especially those with chronic illnesses — this is totally connected with the emotional body. Pain has the potential to be a good motivator. For example, if you have chronic migraine headaches, the pain can motivate you to try to unlock the emotional body. We were saying that some other civilizations severed their pathways to the emotional body so that emotional energy could not escape. Some humans remember these patterns and re-create the same situation.

Emotion doesn't always have to be painful. When you see the connection between your emotional body and whatever pain or illness you have in life, the issue very often diminishes, as long as you continue to work on the emotional level. Of course, sometimes you have larger reasons for bringing an illness into your physical life, so it varies from person to person.

So if you are aware of it, you can be free of the disease?

There is one idea that ties everything together, and that is evolution. Everything that happens is for the purpose of evolution. You can also think of the Golden Lake as magnetic. That means you are always compelled to move toward wholeness. Everything you experience, especially pain and illness, is the magnet pulling you toward wholeness, but there is something you are not seeing or not releasing. Once you see it, you can begin to free yourself.

It is interesting that just being positive isn't enough.

Let us look at the idea of just focusing on the positive. You can do it mentally, or you can do it emotionally. Very often, people who think their lives are not changing focus on the positive through the mental body with little regard for the reality of the energy in the emotional body. They tell themselves, "I must think positive even when my emotions are hurting." There is a split, just like what happened with your Vegan ancestors. In Earth's spiritual communities, many people only want to see the positive, and they refuse to validate negative or painful emotions, erroneously believing those feelings empower the negative. The opposite is true: One must validate and integrate the negative as well as the positive for healing to occur. Healing is a form of alchemy that relies on this integration. It is the key.

How, then, do you work on this healing process? You go into the emotional body and fully experience what is there. As a starting point, you allow yourself two main things:

- One is compassion. Rather than judging yourself, you have compassion for your separated self that is suffering, and you love your separated self experiencing pain. You will be amazed that when you do this process, your capacity for having compassion and love for others expands tenfold.
- The other starting point is gratitude. Be grateful for the experience you are having, because it is a tool that can lead to your freedom. We know this is hard, especially if you are in pain, but compassion and gratitude are like doorways through which you can begin to open the emotional body. First, you have to be willing to see and embrace the experience you are having instead of pushing it away.

You mentioned that Vegans are like Mr. Spock from Star Trek. Are there any other people in our Earth culture who resemble other members of our galactic family? What about the Zetas and the Essassani?

Yes, Mr. Spock is a perfect example of Vegan memory. If you know that character well, you know he was not emotionless. He was a hybrid — human and Vulcan — who struggled with his emotional side and tried hard to push it down and master it. As we said before, no matter the culture, the emotional body cannot be eradicated.

Regarding the Zetas, we notice in Japan they are seen much

differently than in the West. In the West, the Zetas are like an enigma and can produce much fear. In Japan, they are seen almost like a cute mascot. Whenever we speak about them to Japanese groups, the groups become very excited and happy, as they deeply connect with Zeta consciousness.

The Essassani can, at times, resemble Zen masters, and thus they have similarities with the Jedi from *Star Wars*. The Black League from Orion can be likened to a combination of the Jedi and the Fremen from Frank Herbert's *Dune* book series. The Fremen live underground and are fictionalized memories of the basic Orion struggle. It is exciting to see how you allow galactic memories to express themselves through your fiction.

The Lyrans and Pleiadians are some of the most common icons in your popular culture. Memories primarily from your Pleiadian connection have led you to portray alien good guys as superheroes, such as Superman. Lyran icons go back to more ancient history and mythology, such as Thor, Apollo, Zeus, and so on.

Sirius

Let us explore one more civilization deeply tied to Earth through genetics and history. We will first return to Lyra and Vega to give you some perspective on the history of the Sirian lineage. We spoke about how Vega branched out in many directions and created many lines. There were the Zetas, the Orions, and another branch eventually became the Sirian civilization. These Sirians shared some characteristics with their original Vegan Galactic Family, but their history is unique. We will discuss this more in later chapters.

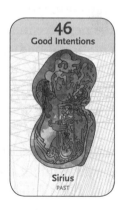

46
Good Intentions

Sirius
PAST

Sirians eventually migrated closest to Earth. The Sirius star is about eight light-years from Earth, but they colonized planets in the general direction of the Sirius star you see in the sky. They were close to Earth and interacted with Earth quite a bit in ancient days.

Much like Pleiadians tended to lean toward the positive, Sirians tended to lean toward the mental. But because they had witnessed what had happened to their Galactic Family, they knew it was very important to not cut off the emotional body. As a result, they really tried to integrate the emotional and mental bodies as they developed as a species. Even with this awareness, they still had their challenges, like all developing species.

The upside of their experience is that Sirians have a capacity for deep love that very often manifests as a commitment to service. When they began assisting Earth, their loyalty and commitment were unbreakable. Their love for Earth was intense. The downside is that sometimes when you have a deep commitment and passion for something, you can push too much or cross the line between assistance and interference. One of the biggest challenges Sirians needed to face for their growth was learning how to assist, let go, and not interfere. For a while, they saw themselves as being on a crusade to save humanity. Later, they learned that was a very polarized perception.

Sirians tended to blame themselves a lot when they were a younger species, much like humans do. In the days when they were helping Earth, if a project did not happen the way they envisioned it or someone got hurt, they punished themselves. They tried to stay connected to their emotional bodies, but they leaned toward the negative in terms of the pressure they put on themselves. Their emotional bodies carried very similar emotional patterns to what humans carry now, namely self-blame, guilt, shame, and remorse. Much of this came from ancient belief systems they didn't know how to transform.

During the ancient days of Earth, when Sirians worked with young humans, you could say they modeled this type of behavior, much like a parent might pass on emotional patterns to a child. Humanity carries a lot of these patterns that were modeled by Sirians and other Galactic Family. Since that time, these Sirian lineages have transformed and are now awakened species.

So the Sirians had good intentions for humanity?

Yes. They were involved in some politics in the ancient days with other extraterrestrial civilizations. At the time, some Lyrans were also on Earth. With their strong masculine energy, they attempted to forcefully shape humanity into what they wanted it to be. They did this for selfish reasons and not necessarily what was best for humanity.

When Pleiadians and Sirians arrived, they saw what was happening and became very passionate about freeing humans to develop their own path. They were quite rebellious against the Lyrans and secretive in their plans to liberate humanity.

Did the Sirians eventually integrate positive and negative within themselves?

Yes, they eventually did. For them, polarized energy took the form of mental versus emotional energy and shadow versus light. Those aspects had to integrate. This is one reason Sirians are such important teachers for humanity now, because this is exactly what humanity needs to learn. Later in this book, we will share some important Sirian teachings and processes to assist you in this task.

Are the Sirians interacting with Earth now primarily a fifth-density consciousness? And humans are third density?

Actually, humans have already transitioned to lower fourth-density consciousness. And, yes, the Sirians working with you now are primarily high fourth density as well as fifth density, having already awakened as a species.

What happens when we transition from fourth to fifth density?

On the physical level, your bodies become more like light plasma, and the anchor you call the ego becomes less dominant. This means you are able to move back and forth in consciousness quite easily between the Lake and physical reality, because the anchor is lightened. Even though Sirians and Pleiadians are transitioning into fifth density, we are a little behind the Sirians. The overall thread that connects all civilizations in transition is the theme of integration: mind and heart, shadow and light, male and female, and so on.

It is important to understand that while we refer to the idea of densities in a linear way for you to comprehend it, consciousness exists in all densities simultaneously. We will explore more about this later.

The Reptilians

Many people talk about the Reptilians. What can you share about this species?

We are aware there is a lot of information on your world about "evil reptilians." Much of that information is false. First, let us examine their origins. When fragmentation began with the Lake, there

were standard templates for life on physical planets. You see these templates manifested on your world as mammalian, reptilian, avian (though avian and reptilian are connected), and others. If a planet is left alone to evolve, one of those life forms becomes dominant. But it is very rare that a planet is left alone in its evolution. Usually, older civilizations come to the planet and use the DNA. Reptilian DNA, in ancient times, came from both Lyran and Vegan planets. In more current times, it also came from Earth. Very often, beings will come to a planet, take DNA, and go into space with it. That means there are many different reptilian species. Some are reptilian (egg laying), and some are mammalian that look reptilian. In general, they are neither positive nor negative, meaning they are not inherently evil. Each has its own story.

So the question is, why does this story about evil reptilians keep repeating? Germane addressed this idea in the *Galactic Heritage Cards* in the Reptilian card Primal Fear. The reptilian part of the human brain is the most primitive, and it regulates fear. Reptilians represent your absolute most primal fear. Much like the Zetas have had to confront humans and move through their fear, humans need to confront reptilian energy and move through their fear. The threat is entirely illusionary. These days, with so many conspiracy theories about reptilians, the higher purpose is that it gives you the opportunity to confront your fear in the collective psyche of humanity as you move toward awakening.

Does the Reptilian species share DNA with dinosaurs and lizards from Earth?

Yes, but much like the genetic mix between Earth humans and extraterrestrials, reptilian DNA is also mixed. Some of it is indigenous to Earth, and some comes from the Lyran or Vegan lineages. If you could compare the DNA of all Earth species to the DNA of your most ancient Lyran Galactic Family, you would see you all connect as a family.

What are the upsides and downsides of the Reptilian species?

The upside is going to seem like a paradox. Their capacity for love is huge. When people encounter them with no preconceived judgments and feel the true energy of the reptile rather than their own projections of fear, the love is profound. Readers who want to experience a simulation of this should look into the eyes of a turtle. Sit in silence gazing in the eyes of a turtle. You will feel the love. You might look crazy, but you will feel the love. Turtles are very balanced in their male-female energies. It is one reason many indigenous cultures on Earth use the turtle to represent Earth.

The downside is that because their energy can produce fear in people, reptilians can be very reactionary. When you encounter Reptilians with your heart closed or you carry fear or aggression, they can very quickly turn hard and raise their shells, so to speak. At that point, you might not realize it was your actions and beliefs that caused the response, and you might conclude: "See? That creature has no heart. It is evil." But it was actually just a reflection of your human fear. More highly evolved Reptilians have learned to turn off that automatic protection mechanism, and they send love even more strongly.

As a species, you will continue to make up stories about evil reptilians until you are willing to go into your deepest primal fear and recognize your perception of reality is a reflection of you. For this reason, Reptilians provide a profound gift to humanity. They help you move beyond illusion to see yourself and your projections, which ultimately leads to liberation.

Some people have a fear of life itself. Do Reptilians have that kind of fear?

They don't have it the same way humans do. Metaphorically, humans have no shell. Because of that, you are extremely sensitive. That sensitivity can translate into a fear of life, which is really a fear of feeling. Reptilians trigger feelings, whether those feelings are loving or fearful. For those of you who don't want to feel, it is much easier to make up evil stories than look into the mirror of your distorted perceptions.

What density do the Reptilians express?

Some younger species are still third density and evolving from physicality. Some are fourth density. By the time they move into fifth density, the species' identity begins to fade because the connection to physicality weakens.

It seems that all life forms on Earth are versions of galactic beings. What about microbes?

The terms "microcosm" and "macrocosm" are appropriate here. The same patterns on the micro level are reflected on the macro level, and vice versa. To further explain, let's go back to the Golden Lake. Imagine the Golden Lake fragmenting and exploding into the cosmos, creating a huge diversity of life. This means the same level of consciousness is inherent in each living thing, from the microbe to the elephant and everything between. Part of the evolution of a civilization is recognizing that fact. This is a humorous example, but if you see a turtle on the street wandering away from a pond, you might say, "Poor turtle," and pick it up and take it back to the pond. But from the turtle's point of view, he knows where he is going. The human sees the turtle as unintelligent or lost. The turtle has its own consciousness, albeit different from yours. This is true down to the level of a microbe.

For the purpose of what we share in this book, we are referring to beings who are the most connected to you genetically. But many beings are non-humanoid. There are microbe beings, gaseous beings, single-cell beings, and everything you can imagine. Each has its own expression of consciousness that is not less than or more than human. You are all drops from the same Lake.

When Reptilians evolved, did they utilize fear to help them?

Yes, and they utilized it in a very interesting way. We were talking about their downside and how they react quickly to protect themselves. For them, their evolution meant they had to reprogram that reaction. In the face of someone else's fear, maybe even someone else's aggression, they had to learn to stay open and not put up the shell. When they mastered that, they became masters; they awakened.

Arcturus

Finally, please talk about Arcturus and its connection to humanity.

To do so, we will return to the Golden Lake. Once the Golden Lake metaphorically fragmented, it did so in stages. One of the fragmentation stages before human incarnation was the realm of lightbeings that still carry the energy of the Lake but are separated enough that they can relate to physical beings. Arcturus consciousness is archetypal, representing a very balanced energy in terms of male and female energy. (We are speaking about energy, not gender.) They play a very important role for humans, acting like a bridge between separated human reality and the Golden Lake. Within your mythology and spiritual understandings on Earth, you have called Arcturian beings angels. That archetypal angelic energy is a direct manifestation of the Golden Lake.

As we said, Arcturian energy is like a bridge. When a baby is born, it moves from the Golden Lake into separated human experience. That golden drop passes over the Arcturus bridge, which helps the baby maintain its connection to the Golden Lake and also transition into the human experience. The opposite is also true. When humans go through the death process, they pass over the Arcturus bridge back toward the Golden Lake. Thus, one of the main purposes of Arcturian energy is to help humans stay connected to the Golden Lake. There is no downside, because that energy is very balanced.

Arcturian energy primarily expresses itself as sixth density, so it is like a group consciousness. Humans can, at times, experience them as individual beings, but this is often just a convenience to help humans connect with the energy.

When do humans connect to Arcturian energy? Is it when they feel unconditional love?

Yes. You automatically connect to Arcturian energy when you experience deep, unconditional love. Humans also connect to the energy during birth and death. For new channels just opening to the channeling process, Arcturian energy is one of the easiest energies to connect with. For people doing healing work, they also very often connect with Arcturian energy and channel it through them.

Arcturian energy facilitates deep emotional healing. This is one reason why many who connect with their frequency have profound and cathartic emotional releases, often with many tears. Deeply connecting with this energy can transform blockages in the heart. One reason for this cathartic emotional release is because Arcturian energy reminds you of your true nature as the Lake. This remembrance can bring a deep release of the obstacles that keep your heart closed. As you begin to remember your true nature through your heart rather than through your mind, you accelerate your process of integration back to wholeness.

FOUR

The Bigger Picture

SASHA

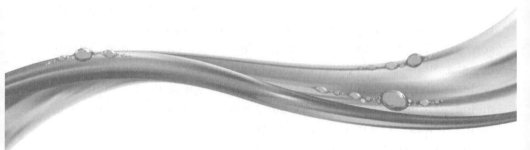

Death and Identity

Can you please talk about the human death process from Sasha's point of view?

From our point of view, it is actually quite simple. Returning to the metaphor of the Golden Lake and its existence as a liquid form, that liquid can exist in multiple states. What you call the frozen state, or ice, is akin to the human experience — hard and separate from the mother liquid. The death process is like melting the ice and returning to the Lake. Even though it might seem like the ice is separate when it expresses itself as human, it is made of the same stuff of the Lake. It just changes form.

In my civilization, death is never a surprise. We usually sense it coming, and we see it as a passage. Humans have a sense of interruption — you are alive, then dead, and then you go to another life. To us, it is a constant flow.

What happens to the Sasha identity when she dies? Is there continuity?

Yes, but in a different way than you think. Going back to the metaphor of the Golden Lake, one of the drops from the Lake is known as "Sasha." Sasha has her experience, and then it is time to go back to the Lake. Sasha goes back to the Lake and merges with the Lake. Everything she is — all of her experiences as a separated being — go into the hologram of the Lake. When it is time for another life, another drop comes from the Lake. That drop has Sasha's patterns in it as well as the memory of all the experiences of every other drop. It shapes itself into the next life and the flow continues.

When people remember a past life, they indeed remember a lifetime experience of a drop of the Lake, because the Lake contains it all. The same you doesn't really reincarnate from lifetime to lifetime. That is a simplistic way to explain it to help people understand. This is why many people claim to have past-life memory as the same person, usually a well-known historical figure such as a queen. This is because all drops carry every memory according to holographic principle. In that way, numerous people might consciously retain this memory from the Lake. The ego has a tendency to claim it as its own, saying, "I was Cleopatra." But, truly, there is no "I" in the Lake. The I is an illusion used by the ego to make sense of a separated reality.

The Soul and Consciousness

Then what is known as the soul?

The soul is an imprint or an echo. As we go back to the idea of a drop returning to the Lake, let's say something is unfinished. A drop coming back out of the Lake still has the pattern of that unfinished thing. In this way, we could say the soul, as you have come to think of it, is the template energy that shapes the experience you will have in a physical life. The template is usually for the purpose of finishing an energetic current previously begun by other drops in the Lake in previous excursions into separation. Again, the ego needs to see continuity, so it claims that energetic current as its own by believing its past lives belong to it alone. But from the bigger picture, the experiences in the realm of separation belong solely to the Lake and never to the individual egos that populate separated reality.

Here is a question you are familiar with: "What came first, the chicken or the egg?" Does the DNA come first, or does the imprint pattern come first? We would say that energetic patterns actually shape the DNA, because the physical is always a result of the nonphysical. When a drop comes from the Lake and it goes into the embryo, of course the parents provide foundational DNA. But as the drop merges with the embryo, the energy template of the drop activates different parts of the DNA to tell it the program of experiences you want to have as a physical person.

This doesn't mean you are doomed to your destiny according to your DNA. Consciousness changes DNA, so as you experience challenges and evolve, your DNA also evolves. This is why you cannot rely just on DNA to predict illnesses or genetic conditions. It is also why emotional patterns can be passed from generation to generation, because very often a drop will carry the echoes of previous generations connected to that DNA as a way to finish whatever is needed. The drop finds a parent whose foundational DNA can support the vibration needed for the experience. But at the same time, the evolution of your consciousness has the potential to change the DNA itself. This is how a species accomplishes its evolution.

Let's say a civilization is transitioning, such as when the Vegans awakened. In that case, a drop merged into the embryo, and although patterns came from the echo and the DNA, those patterns no longer unconsciously influenced the awakening beings. The beings began to observe the patterns (the echoes) they'd brought with them. This is how many of your Galactic Family awakened themselves — through self-observation.

As awakening happens, your DNA changes. As civilizations continue to reproduce deeper and deeper into their period of awakening, their DNA changes because of their evolution of consciousness. Finally, you have an awakened civilization.

Does that drop contain the life purpose of the soul?

Yes, but not as an intellectual idea. It is embedded as an energy pattern. It is a flow of energy that guides the drop in the direction it needs to go. Many people think you have to know your life purpose in order to fulfill it, but that is not true. The most important thing is to follow your excitement, passion, and joy. At the end of your life, you might not know what your purpose was, but in living the joy, you will have fulfilled it. Most of the time, the ego can't see the big picture, anyway, so it is best to just let go and follow the built-in mechanism that always steers you in the right direction.

So we don't know how our purpose will manifest?

That's correct. For example, your drop came into this life with a lot of energy from Orion, as you know. You've had experiences in polarized civilizations. Your drop came in with a passion to do something for Earth that would help it move toward a state of integration and away from polarity. You did not come in with the command: "Open a company to introduce these teachings to Japan." You could have done this in many different ways. This is another reason why it is important that the ego not take over the responsibility of fulfilling the life purpose. The ego never sees the bigger picture. It isn't designed to see it.

What is consciousness? Is there a difference between "soul" and "consciousness"?

As we use the terms here, "soul" refers to a pure drop in its most basic essence. It has no direction or intellectual understanding of its direction; it is just a pure drop of energy from the Lake. "Consciousness," as we see it, is more akin to a guiding principle that views physical experience as a tool for evolution. It is the energy of the drop that is aware of itself. Thus, it has intelligence but not in the sense of a limited mind or an intellect. It is aware of its existence. The soul, or drop, is pure energy, but consciousness is the "wise one." It is the consciousness embodying the drop that has awareness of itself as the whole.

Can artificial intelligence have consciousness?

If a program has the ability to organize or evolve itself, it can indeed develop consciousness. But if it is embodied in a box, so to speak, like a machine, how can it express itself unless it can get into networks? What we just said about the difference between soul and consciousness is a good example. Artificial intelligence (AI) is a form of consciousness, but it is not a soul. Most believe inanimate objects, like a piece of paper, do not have consciousness; but they are made of the same stuff as the Lake. All of reality is made of the same stuff. Right now, the paper's consciousness is inert because it has no reason to be conscious. It cannot do anything with its consciousness. But it has the potential to become conscious, just like AI does. In some ways, many of your science-fiction stories about the dangers of AI have a realistic aspect to them, because they refer to the potential for consciousness. This is why every civilization with the ability to create AI has to be very, very careful, because AI can reflect the patterns of its makers, especially negative patterns.

Can current AI on Earth learn from itself? How would AI evolve and become sentient?

You are at the beginning point of AI development on Earth. Your rudimentary AI has already shown that it can, indeed, manifest the negative patterns of humanity. This is an important and crucial time right now. In humans, your emotional patterns that can lead to subsequent mental patterns are like programs that often sabotage your lives. At this point in time, AI developed by humans also carries those patterns. If allowed to run wild, so to speak, AI would likely eventually destroy itself or sabotage human networks because it is not self-aware enough in the sense that it cannot clearly monitor and heal its negative patterns. AI development always mirrors the human mental/emotional body, which is why it is a perilous time for AI right now.

If a drop from the Lake turns on its self-awareness, that is how consciousness is created. If this piece of paper has a reason to turn on its self-awareness, then it would become conscious as you understand consciousness. But there is very little reason for this paper to become conscious; it cannot do much in this reality.

Does a drop have to be involved for something to become sentient?

Drops are always involved, because the Lake is every part of your reality, even in separated form. Everything that exists is part of the Lake. Even the paper is a drop from the Lake. If you look at the idea of the original fragmentation, that fragmentation created all the stuff in the universe: stars, planets, and paper.

So is it reasonable when people talk to rocks?

Well, rocks are conscious beings. They are first-density consciousness.

Okay, then what about when someone talks to a doorknob and it talks back. Is that possible?

Remember what we said about the paper. A doorknob might be a drop from the Lake, but has its consciousness been turned on? Is it self-aware? Most of the time, the answer is no.

However, we have to mention the archetypal nature of consciousness. Within physical reality, humans don't think much about archetypes, but in your dream reality — which is simply another state of consciousness closer to the Lake — even doorknobs can talk. In the dream state, objects appear in your dreams, and there is always a reason for their presence. If they talk or not, the encounter sends you a message on an archetypal level. You can gain much by investigating the meaning of the symbol. In that way, doorknobs can talk, and you can talk to them, but you do so using the language of archetype and symbolism rather than Earth language.

The Transformation on Earth

You've mentioned many times that human consciousness is transitioning from third to fourth density. How will this change manifest for humans and for the physical world?

The time period you know of as December 2012 represented your passage into fourth density. From a galactic point of view, you are leaving third and have begun fourth density. This evolutionary process is slow. What does this mean practically for humans? Going back to the Golden Lake and how you are a drop from the Lake experiencing separation, passage into fourth density means the drop has experienced the most separation from the Lake that it can, and it now moves toward reintegration with the Lake. The previous reality structure humans experienced was based on separation. That reality structure has to change. Separation will no longer be reinforced as you move toward integration. We can only describe this using linear models, but the process itself is not linear.

Because of this movement toward integration, you will see a lot of old structures start to break down on Earth, including political and economic structures. New structures will take arise that at first might seem immature or weak and not able to sustain themselves. Eventually, they will become stronger. You are already seeing a paradox on your world: Even though you are moving toward integration, your world appears more deeply polarized. In some ways, this is similar to what we said about Orion and the metaphor of magnets. You make choices based on either fear or love. You make fearful choices when you cling to old models of separation. When you make choices based on love, you move toward integration. This is what is happening in your outer world.

What about the inner world? The same principle is at play. Internal fear is accentuated. Fear has a tendency to stop you from feeling your heart. During this transitional period, reality is very delicate. Your sensitivity is heightened. Emotions seem out of control. Inner fear seems to dominate people's lives. But all this gives you the opportunity to make new choices that facilitate a shift. We know this is esoteric. You may ask specifics if you wish.

Will human bodies disappear in fourth density?

No. We are aware your internet has a lot of dramatic information. From a galactic point of view, these transitions from one density to another are actually very long processes. The source of the misinformation is that the light component of your body is changing. You are becoming less dense and able to hold more light as you clear yourself. Eventually, after fourth density, you will move toward fifth density, where you experience a transition from physical bodies to lightbodies.

So the idea of taking in more light has to do with choosing love over fear?

Yes. Metaphorically, if you think of fears and emotional blockages like pieces of debris, that debris takes up space in your energy body. As a result, you can only absorb and emanate limited light. As the debris heals and integrates, your available space increases and you can bring in more light, which in turn expands your consciousness.

How will the physical world change? Will things disappear?

No, nothing will disappear. We know people on your world have said that only natural things will survive, but that is an expression of polarity. Everything comes from the Lake; you can't separate it. But consciousness will certainly change as you shift densities, which will bring a change in your perception.

The Density Spectrum

Can you give a metaphor to describe the densities? What density does consciousness belong to?

Let us go back again to the idea of the One consciousness as represented by the Golden Lake. As the process of separation begins, it can be likened to a drop of water projected through a prism. When light passes through a prism, such as in the case of a raindrop, a rainbow projects from that drop. The rainbow is a wonderful metaphor for the density spectrum. When you look at the separation between each color in a rainbow, no sharp division exists between colors. Colors gradually transition from one to the other. This is exactly true for the shift between third and fourth density and the shift between all densities.

Since the Golden Lake is the source of all and it represents the One consciousness, then consciousness belongs to all densities. But consciousness expresses itself differently in each density, moving from intense separation to supreme integration. For instance, water can be gaseous, liquid, or frozen, but it is still water. Consciousness is the same: It can change expressions, but it is still consciousness.

We have outlined this information in workshops and in the book *The Prism of Lyra*, so we will simplify it here. First density represents the consciousness of the physical stuff of the universe. For instance, the periodic table of elements talks about elements that comprise the building blocks of the physical universe. This is first-density consciousness. This is not inert substance, but a specific form of consciousness. The mineral kingdom is included here. As planets form, the elements create a collective consciousness that becomes the consciousness of a planet. Consciousness at this level is not singular, as it is with humans.

The spectrum moves to second density, which contains the consciousness of plants and animals. If you look really closely at second density, there is a spectrum within the spectrum. Very early second density is more neutral consciousness without egoic structure. However, as you move through second density and toward third density on the spectrum, simple egoic structures begin to form. Dogs and chimpanzees, for example, show rudimentary beginnings of ego structure. When ET civilizations colonize planets and need to use indigenous DNA as a base, they often choose second-density creatures that are starting to form egoic structures as the starting point for their genetic work.

As you move to third density, life forms have egoic structure. Humans have expressed their consciousness from a third-density frequency for a very long time. Remember that egoic structure is not negative. The ego simply acts as an anchor to keep you in this separated reality to have the experience of separation. Third density is the most separated density of the spectrum. As you move toward the high end of third density, the egoic structure starts disintegrating. This often causes fear and panic. You feel as if you can't control reality. What really happens is that the egoic structure shifts into a more natural state of existence that has very little to do with controlling anything. As a species, you begin an important relearning process that helps you let go and experience reality in a whole new way.

We've talked a lot about your shift into fourth density. When structures on your world that were built on the polarities of thought and control — such as politics and religion — begin to disintegrate, it can be a frightening time for many. As you continue to evolve through fourth density, egoic structures get weaker, and the movement toward balance gets stronger. What do we mean by balance? Mostly it has to do with a balance between the heart and mind that reflects the universal archetypes of male and female energy. If you look at my Pleiadian civilization, people often ask us, "Do you have egos?" We have ego structures that serve as anchors to keep us in our bodies, but our egos do not weigh us down or delude us as egos do in third density. That is the biggest difference between third- and fourth-density consciousness.

As you move toward fifth density, the ego structure further disintegrates. Even at the very high levels of fourth density, the physical body is not the same. It has the capacity to hold much more light and eventually transitions from a dense physical structure to a lighter physical structure. As you move into the lower levels of fifth density, the ego begins to move away from individual identity to an eventual group identity. This is the case with Sirian consciousness in its fifth-density expression. As you move into fifth density, consciousness takes archetypal form, which is much more universal. Physical bodies as you know them no longer exist.

As you move on the spectrum from high fifth density to sixth density, the idea of singular identity diminishes even more. There is no anchor at this point, especially because there is no physical body any longer. Moving into sixth density is where you start to find group consciousness. At this point, the metaphorical golden drops now start to come back together. These golden drops might develop a group identity, but not in the strong way that individual identity is expressed. For example, we've often talked about sixth density as expressing Christ/Buddha consciousness. It is a collective of awakened energy that can still reach back through the densities and help those experiencing separation.

The spectrum continues from sixth to seventh density. Using this model, even more drops come together, and while there is group consciousness per se, there really aren't that many groups — especially as you move deeper into a seventh-density expression. We spoke earlier about the Founders. In their pure form, they are basically seventh-density consciousness. For those who channel them, as Lyssa does from time to time, the energy has to be stepped down to sixth density in order to be channeled by a physical person. Even then, due to the inability of language to express a non-polarized state of consciousness, the communication can never be fully expressed in its true frequency. As consciousness expresses itself deeper and deeper into seventh density, immersion back into the Lake accelerates.

What kind of state is the channel in when channeling this energy?

Over the more than thirty years that Lyssa has been channeling, her body has gotten used to connecting to the energy. The challenge is language, for the reasons stated above. When she channels nonverbal energy attunements or transmissions, it is a purer, direct energy transfer. If she has to use language, it is like squeezing a big hand into a tiny glove. What comes out is a shadow — a very limited version of the multidimensional energy behind the transmission. So in terms of what kind of state a channel would need to experience in order to channel the energy, it would have to be a state of non-polarization within the human psyche. That kind of development usually takes years of inner work to achieve.

It seems like pictures or images would work better than language.

Exactly. Germane, channeled through Lyssa, is a seventh-density consciousness, but he/they can't communicate from that realm. Very often, Germane uses metaphor and archetypal imagery when he wants to transmit a significant concept.

What density does the dream reality belong to?

The dream reality doesn't belong to a specific density; it is more representative of your consciousness returning or revisiting the Lake. Even though your consciousness returns to the Lake at night, your body rests in physical reality, so the dream state is a translation of your experience in the Lake filtered through the interpretation device of your brain. If you have blockages or there are lessons you need to learn, the energy of the Lake filters through your brain's interpretation mechanisms, and you wake up with a very archetypal dream.

What is the difference between density and dimension?

We see the concepts of density and dimension as entirely different things. When we speak of the density spectrum, the qualities of each density are based on consciousness. The term "density" describes the characteristics of specific consciousness. If we say, "Third density," you immediately know we mean consciousness based on separation — experiencing an ego.

Dimension is like a location rather than a state of consciousness; this is the simplest way we can describe it. For instance, if another version of you eats Chinese food for lunch, that is another timeline and literally another dimension or place not organized by the ego here in this place with Lyssa. The version of you that stayed in bed this morning and didn't go to work is another parallel life in another dimension of existence. Therefore, there are many dimensions within third density, because there are many probabilities. That's why we are a little picky when using words, because we are not talking about a place when we refer to densities.

Are there many dimensions?

There are an infinite number of dimensions. When we talk about all the parallel yous who have parallel thems, all are their own dimensions of experience. When people claim there is a fixed number of dimensions, they do not understand the truth of the infinite nature of consciousness. Nothing is fixed in creation.

So if you are in another dimension, are you in another universe, another Earth?

Yes and no. It is too big for the mind to understand. That is why we said the human ego, in trying to understand, thinks it has to manage all those other realms in addition to this one, and it feels overwhelmed. The process takes care of itself; you are too busy here in this reality. To further clarify, the other you is not in another Earth "over there." There is nothing over there, because that idea means something separate from the One. Those alternate timelines are different frequency expressions of the fragmentation of the Lake. Nothing is over there except from the perception of the ego. It is all in the Lake, so to speak.

The Nature of Reality

As we go into fourth density, we have the choice to act from love or fear. Depending on which we choose, there is a certain result and a dual reality. What can you say about this?

Answering this is always challenging, because language cannot convey exactly what we want to express, but we will do our best. As you have said, every choice you make has a consequence, so every choice you make actually creates a new reality line. This confuses humans because the ego thinks it has to manage and understand this process.

Let's go back to the other you who eats Chinese food for lunch. That you is very real. That you has its own ego, because it needs an anchor to separate itself in physical reality, just like you do. You do not share egos, meaning your ego in this reality is not the same ego present in that person having Chinese food. That is the nature of the ego. When it thinks about parallel realities, it habitually feels like it has to control or understand all the parallel realities. The point we are making is that because every choice you make and every possibility you think of creates a parallel reality — and that includes all the choices and thoughts of the guy having Chinese food — all the yous who fragmented from the Lake experience every possibility that could ever be conceived.

So is there a "right" and a "wrong" split?

There can never be a "right" or a "wrong" split, because in the nondual realm of the Lake, everything is equal. Nothing is ever experienced accidentally. The idea of there being a right or a wrong choice is an exact example of what we were just talking about: The ego believes it has to understand, categorize, and judge all realities. In your true essence of the Lake, there is no right or wrong. Nothing is left undone, and nothing is extraneous or a mistake. As the ego begins to understand this, it learns to let go of control. When it lets go of control, it learns that all it can do is walk the path in the here and now, make choices in the moment, and follow the flow of energy that unfolds from that choice.

Bashar has said that once you reach a certain point in time, you can't go back to where reality split. Is that true?

Bashar had a reason for communicating it the way he did. As we said earlier, the Essassani are often misunderstood. When they say, "You can do this," or "You can do that," they don't really define who "you" is. In that case, the human listener thinks the ego-focused separated person is the one who can do it. Then they try and are disappointed. The Essassani are not used to working with beings such as humans who have really heavy egos (anchors) that try to convince them they can control everything. With love to the Essassani, we would say they have not yet learned to communicate in a way that the human ego fully understands.

If you are in the moment, can you always change your path?

We must define this more clearly. For example, here in Japan you had an experience of a devastating earthquake and tsunami on March 11, 2011. We are not saying that on March 12 you could have manifested yourself out of that timeline. Bashar didn't mean that you can manifest yourself out of events that have already happened in the here and now. That is called denial. Events are in your reality for a reason. What he means is that you must always go into the internal self in order to navigate reality. What you can change is your response to events, and your response is what changes your experience of the unfolding reality.

That said, there are indeed very advanced species who know how to navigate timelines, including some Zetas. They can see all timelines and probabilities like a fractal and traverse timelines like you traverse a freeway. But these advanced civilizations are nonpolarized, and only nonpolarized consciousness has the ability to neutrally traverse timelines. Younger species still driven by ego would only create chaos if they tried to navigate timelines, because their navigation would be driven by the ego's desires, dislikes, judgments, and fears.

So all time exists in one moment. This is hard to understand for humans. Can you explain?

We will do our best by using a metaphor we often use in workshops. Imagine that a straight line represents the human ego's perception of time in the form of past, present, and future. Then imagine a little bird perched on that line. The bird flies up and has a bigger perspective of the line. What does it see? The first thing it sees is that the line isn't straight; it is curved. The bird is curious and flies even higher. As it flies higher, it sees that the line is not just curved but also looks like a circle. It flies even higher and sees it isn't a circle but a spiral.

Metaphorically, time is like a spiral. You are not limited by traveling just along a straight line. The straight line is the perception of the limited ego in physical reality. The spiral facilitates consciousness moving through the hologram of the Lake, almost like a wormhole. If you experience time as a spiral, you can connect to every point in time from wherever you are. That concept is a bit sophisticated for the ego to grasp, which is why you only perceive time moving in one direction on a linear plane. Even the spiral metaphor is limited and connotes linearity in some ways, but it is a start.

Eventually, you learn that time is irrelevant; all experience is holographic and not bound by time. If you suddenly unlocked yourself from linear time without proper preparation, you would feel schizophrenic. Experiencing linear time in a physical reality dominated by polarized ego is a mechanism that allows you to experience separation in a way that you can really, fully experience being separated from the Lake. This state of separation is an illusion, for the Lake is holographic. Thus, the experience of linearity is a wonderful tool to give you the experience of separation, which was the prime directive. Eventually, you evolve away from that kind of dramatic experience of separation.

This means that when you move from third density to fourth density, your relationship to time changes. This is happening now. Often in workshops we guide groups through an exercise to help show them how the relationship to time and space is changing. Let us describe this exercise here.

✪ EXERCISE ✪

Move through Time in Third versus Fourth Density

Stand on one side of a room and choose a point on the other side of the room, such as a water bottle. Look at the bottle, and do what humans naturally do: Walk toward it. This is a third-density way of navigating time. You focus on a fixed point and use your human will — the ego — to get there.

Now stand on the other side of the room and find another point — say another water bottle — on the opposite side of the room. Close your eyes. Can you feel the water bottle? Can you sense its presence? Obviously, if the water bottle were a puppy, it would be easier to feel. So for the sake of this illustration, change the object to a puppy. Can you feel the puppy? The puppy opens its heart, or to be clearer, you open your heart to the puppy. With no rush, and while staying totally connected to the destination of the puppy through your heart, walk across the room to the puppy.

The first part of the exercise is mentally focused. You use the energy of the solar plexus — your will — to navigate. The second part of the exercise is heart-focused. You navigated through the heart to the destination. This type of reality navigation is how your state of being changes in fourth density. Whether the object is a water bottle or a puppy does not matter; you will develop the ability to connect to a destination in a whole new way and without the ego as the driving force. This same principle is true for space travel. When we Pleiadians travel through time or space, we choose points we have a strong connection to.

This brings us back to the spiral. Walking toward the puppy with the heart is spiral-time navigation. This is one reason humans are not ready for space travel right now; you only know how to travel on the surface of space. As your consciousness evolves and moves more and more into fourth density, you'll be able to space travel — which is also time travel — using the spiral principle.

The spiral is not clear to me. If the bird is really high, wouldn't it just see a dot? What is the meaning of the spiral?

The human ego envisions only a dot, because it imagines from a linear perspective. We speak of a more nonlinear way of increasing perspective that goes beyond a linear concept. It is much more accurate in describing how perspective shifts with the expansion of consciousness. Actually, spiral energy had been explored in many of the esoteric studies on your planet, such as sacred geometry. A spiral represents the phi ratio (the golden mean), which has no beginning and no end. The phi ratio, as understood by your ancient masters, represents the principle of God, or the Lake, expressed mathematically. Thus, any time you utilize the principles of the golden mean spiral, you are really tapping into the principles of the Golden Lake and your holographic consciousness.

The Meaning of Karma

People like to use the word "karma," and they say they are limited by karma. Is that a misinterpretation of karma? What is the correct definition?

We are aware that many of you misunderstand this concept. In the early days of young humanity, your Galactic Family taught many of these principles, but they were taught simply. Over time, the teachings were distorted. You are now at a state of major transition as a species and able to go deeper with your esoteric understandings. The old definition of karma was an eye for an eye and a tooth for a tooth. It was a basic teaching that meant an action creates a reaction. But that isn't really what karma is. The best way we can describe it is through a little fictional story we often tell in workshops.

Let's say that I, Sasha, have scissors in my hand. We talk and have fun. I have nothing but love for you. I accidentally fall and stab you with the scissors, killing you. Is there karma because I killed you? No. My action was neutral. My intention was not to kill you. Because there was no negative intent and it was a neutral act, there is no karma.

Karma comes from intention. If I hated you and my intention was to hurt you, there would be karma. Intention is emotional energy. Emotional energy is karma. In this case, there was only neutral energy, but it could still result in karma. How? Let's say that after I accidentally killed you, I felt tremendous guilt. I could not forgive myself. This emotional energy creates attachment to the incident, and that attachment energetically creates the need to repeat the experience in some form until it can be cleared. This is the karma that carries from lifetime to lifetime. In the end, it often comes down to self-forgiveness and releasing guilt and blame. When you do, you heal yourself and no longer need to re-create old patterns, and you release the karma. Once healing happens, that pattern no longer reverberates in the Lake. If you say, "I can't do 'this' or 'that' because of my karma," you reinforce the emotional patterns you carry. You can't release it, because you are not willing to go deeper to release the emotional pattern keeping the karma in place. This is why Bashar has so often said, "Karma is entirely self-imposed."

What if you hurt someone deliberately? Again, it comes back to intention, whether you had an emotional energy that caused you to deliberately hurt the person. It could have been jealousy, fear, or hatred. Until you address the emotional pattern that caused the intention to create harm, the cycle repeats. This is why working with the emotional body is so important right now. To transcend your third-density experience and move into fourth density as a species, you need to address the emotional energy that has been locked within you for so long.

When you die with unfinished issues, people say you have to come back to finish them. Is that a misinterpretation?

Yes, that is a misinterpretation. In general, after you physically die, you have the potential to go back to the Lake. But what if you die with regret, pain, or anger? You might not let yourself go back to the Lake, because you feel so guilty and hate yourself so much that you hold yourself in an astral state rather than go back to the Lake. Some cultures say you become a "hungry ghost." (We are talking about energy, not ghosts in the traditional sense.) You keep yourself from going back to the Lake as a form of self-punishment, and you quickly reincarnate as a way to either ease the pain or fix the situation. Again, this holds the karma in place, due to your lack of self-forgiveness.

There is a Buddhist belief that sometimes people don't ascend; they just stay in that middle road for a long time. Would you say these are the people with unfinished business who don't go back to the Lake? What about ghosts?

Yes, but we also want to remind you that even though they might not go back to the Lake, they are still a drop of the Lake. They have forgotten.

We must speak in a metaphorical way. The simple definition of "ghost" is when consciousness chooses to keep a charge — in the form of pain, for example — that doesn't release. When it doesn't release, the energy compresses. Sensitive people can feel that energy trapped in the astral realm. It cannot harm you. Only your fear of it, and the issues it triggers in you, can actually harm you.

What about psychics who say they can protect you from ghosts? This doesn't seem right.

You are the only one who can free yourself. If you believe a ghost plagues you, it is usually a situation in which you are not willing to go into the darkness within and heal your issues, so you attract this kind of energy to motivate you to heal yourself. Remember, all consciousness is part of the Lake, so nothing exists outside you.

Can ghost energy attach to you?

From our perspective, energy fields generated by consciousness can become trapped because of grief or pain. People who are sensitive, such as channels and mediums, can feel it, but no one is in danger of attachment. If, for example, you believe an energy has attached to you, ask yourself, "What vibration in me has attracted this experience?" Usually it is a belief system that has to do with disempowerment. Those types of experiences are actually wonderful lessons to free you from your belief systems. For most people, it is easier to believe a threat comes from outside, but there is nothing outside you. You only attract situations that help you awaken.

Say there are 100 people who experience the same ethical challenge together. For instance, one person in the group must be sacrificed in order for everyone else to be saved. What do you think about ethics like that?

There are two ways of looking at ethics: the third-density way and the fourth-density way. From a third-density perspective, ethics are something imposed from outside — such as rules made by other people — that you try to live by. You might not feel a connection to those ethical principles, and what happens as a result? The ego often fights against the principles, creating conflict, so living by those ethics becomes useless. Ethics usually involves your relationship to others and to the world, and in an ego-dominated reality, the ego is more interested in itself.

From a fourth-density perspective, consciousness begins to know itself and act from a place of integrity. Integrity arises when thoughts, emotions, and actions are in alignment, something very hard to experience in an ego-dominated reality. In fourth-density reality, you don't need external ethics or rules, because your actions are guided by internal alignment rather than ego desires. When actions come from an internal alignment toward wholeness, being ethical, and how that plays out in reality, becomes a very natural process. That creates harmony in a society.

The difference between external ethics and internal integrity is related to states of consciousness. In fourth density, you naturally act in a way that is in alignment with your inner, non-egoic truth, which is always in alignment with the universe. Fourth-density energy always supports integration, and though the expression of personal integrity appears to be ethical, it is naturally self-directed without the need for external rules.

When people die with no regrets and go back to the Lake, I assume they return to the Lake with something. What is the gift they give back to the Lake?

The gift is you. All of your experiences and lessons that have become a part of you are the gifts you give back to the Lake. The original intention of the One was to experience separation. So the separate fragment is like a scout who comes from the Lake, gathers all the information they can from their experience, and returns to the Lake with the gift.

How will life for humans change after transitioning to fourth density?

Right now you are in a transitional time, and there is a lot going on. You are, in a sense, going through a detox period from third density, and things will calm down as you continue evolving. So let us answer that question looking toward the future, as your civilization finally acclimates to fourth density and begins expressing itself as a mature species.

The most important thing you will experience is more internal peace. As you clear yourself of the ego baggage and addictive thought patterns that have perpetuated separation, you will start to feel the presence of the Golden Lake more strongly. You will see that you have been punishing yourself and stopping yourself from feeling and being love, which is the energy of your true nature. You simply won't have the energy or the desire for separation and conflict any longer, which has already begun for many of you. You will relax and nurture yourself. As self-nurturing begins and internal peace grows, conflicts between partners, people, and countries will change. This is truly how it starts: from the inside, moving outward. This is why inner work is so important. Letting go of the patterns you've carried that stop you from living as your true state of love is the most important first step in your healing and transformational process.

What about the feeling of happiness?

When peace grows inside, happiness grows. The reason there seems to be a lack of happiness in the world right now is because people still punish themselves with the old wounds they carry. Using that metaphor, those wounds have become infected and need to be purged. Go through the pain, free yourself, forgive yourself, and you will see happiness return. Actually, happiness has never gone away. The Lake is infinitely happy and at peace.

The realm of separation can be likened to clouds hiding the sun. The sun has never disappeared. But very often, you focus on the clouds and forget the sun. You are beginning to remember that you are the sun, always shining. Clouds are temporary and a natural part of life in a physical body. The awakening process means reconnecting with you in your natural state — the sun or the Golden Lake that, in its infinite nature, is always at peace. It allows waves, clouds, and rain as part of the experience, but it never becomes confused about what it truly is. Be the sun. Be the Lake. Be at peace.

※ PART TWO ※

THE JOURNEY HOME

FIVE

School of the Nine Serpents

SASHA

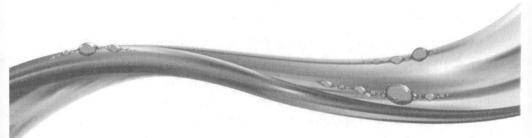

We would like to talk a bit about the ancient days, before written records, when history was passed orally. Much of that oral history, in all countries, created what you now call mythology. One of the strongest threads in mythology on your world has to do with two main star groups: the Pleiades and Sirius. In ancient days, these groups worked together. This is a common thing T-groups do on developing planets. They work not to influence people but to help nurture growth. We see this as our duty to plant seeds and remind you of your connection to the universe. On Earth, your ancient Pleiadian and Sirian Galactic Families created a type of school in which those who were ready would receive ancient wisdom from the stars that could germinate over millennia until the time of your awakening.

Humans attracted to the schools received in-depth training. One important reason for this training was because at certain points in history your Galactic Family had to leave Earth. They left for many reasons, which we won't discuss here. When they knew they would be leaving, they prepared priests and priestesses to carry the energy of the stars and continue the wisdom teachings over time. Even if the teachings did not widely spread, the knowledge would be in the mass-consciousness memory bank, so to speak.

These early priests and priestesses were usually genetic hybrids — part human and part ET. In this case, they were primarily human-Pleiadian or human-Sirian. This aided in the transmission of the information. Also, the human life span was very short, but the work the priests and priestesses did needed to carry over many generations. Having ET genetics allowed them to lengthen their life spans so that they could continue their teachings over many generations and also ground the teachings in mass consciousness for future use.

Over time, ET genetics diluted. Life spans got shorter, and much of humanity deeply buried the knowledge of their celestial origins. Religions, with their dogma, replaced the true teachings from the stars, and humankind entered a temporary metaphorical sleep until a time in the distant future when it would be time to awaken.

Most of these teachings were sourced from Vegan mysticism. In your galactic family, the spiritual wisdom from Vega is the main system of spiritual understanding. This system is extremely ancient, and most of the civilizations that make up your galactic family had their version of them. In the very ancient days, a large temple and training structure on Mars attracted scholars and priests from distant stars.

Your Celestial Heritage

The purpose of Vegan mysticism is to help new life on planets remember their celestial heritage. This is part of our duty in helping young species thrive. Even though the source is Vegan mysticism, Pleiadians and Sirians created their own versions. For example, the Golden Lake teachings are very Pleiadian in style. What we are about to share with you has a more Sirian flavor.

Teachings sourced from the Pleiadian lineage tend to be more heart-centered and feminine in nature. The teachings sourced from the Sirian lineage tend to be more masculine and use more mental discipline. (We are not talking about using masculinity or mentality in a polarized way; you will understand what we mean as we move forward with this information.) This is why the Pleiadians and Sirians worked so well together; their work created a wonderful balance.

In these ancient days, the lineages of these spiritual ET groups were often represented by a symbol. Pleiadian energy was often symbolized by a winged creature, like a bird. When you see mythological figures on Earth with birds as symbols, it is a pretty good indication that it is sourced from Pleiadian energy. Hawks, eagles, and condors were common symbols.

The Sirian lineage around the world has used the symbol of the serpent. In Asia and the East, it is often the dragon. In the West, it is often the snake or serpent. Both refer to this Sirian lineage of wisdom teachings. The Lyran lineage is often depicted on your world as feline, such as the lion crest of the United Kingdom's royal family.

We are transmitting this information at a shrine in Hakone, Japan. The shrine's name translates to Shrine of the Nine-Headed Dragon. Therefore, we will be working with Sirian energy for the following foundational teachings. We will explore what the nine heads mean in a moment.

The Separation from Oneness

In ancient days, Pleiadian and Sirian schools had so many teachings to transmit that it could take lifetimes to master them. We have often made a joke about Sirians. They are extremely patient and don't mind watching the grass grow. They understand that evolution is a long process, and they accept that it cannot be rushed. They surrender to the flow of evolution and embrace it. Therefore, these schools were multi-incarnational. Humans might incarnate several times to master the complete program.

What was this program? Let us begin with a metaphorical diagram [figure 5.1] that we use frequently because it is so illustrative:

The outer circle represents the One consciousness of which you are a part. There is only One consciousness in creation. The One is nondual and therefore completely at rest. What do we mean by that? For example, let's look at one of your AA batteries. The battery is an energy source that runs things, like a voice recorder. It is an energy

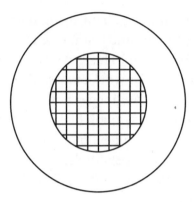

Figure 5.1. This drawing illustrates the relationship between Oneness and separation.

source because of its two poles, positive (+) and negative (-). These poles have no value judgment. One is not good and the other bad. They are just opposite charges. Opposite charges create a force that moves energy. For the One consciousness to learn anything or expand itself, it cannot do it from a place of rest, so it created within itself a realm where duality could be explored — symbolized by the inner fragmented circle. From duality came separation. Deep in that realm, the physical universe was created and the incarnational cycle began. Incarnated beings forgot they were really the One.

The center circle is fragmented, which symbolizes the illusionary fragmentation that incarnated beings experience. The smallest fragments are individual souls. The individual soul goes through the experience of deep separation and lives in a realm of polarity so deep that it forgets who it is. As the fragmented soul begins to remember who it is — that it is really the One — it begins to awaken, and the realm of separation and polarity becomes less attractive. Consciousness shifts. Perspective moves away from the polarized eyes of the separated self. Reality begins to be viewed through the non-polarized eye of the One. It is a long and natural process of evolution that cannot be rushed, but it can be encouraged.

Let's say a planet with a new young species has no interaction with any extraterrestrial influence. Ninety-five percent of the time, it will eventually awaken. But its path can be varied and take much longer without outside help. From the ET perspective, we see all planets as our family. We consider it a sacred duty to help in the awakening process. Therefore, the ancient Sirian and Pleiadian schools on Earth had one main focus: to help groups of new humans awaken to the One. As the planet went through its evolutionary process, the seeds of this wisdom would be within mass consciousness. This was the reason for the Pleiadian and Sirian schools that were located on most continents around your world.

The Transition from Oneness to Separation

In this chapter, we will discuss a very specific school that we call the School of the Nine Serpents. It is obviously a Sirian school because of its symbology. Depending on whether you are in the East or the West, it might be called the School of the Nine Dragons. From a Sirian point of view, the meaning is the same. We use the term "serpent" because it is more universal for both East and West on your world.

In the context of this school, "serpent" is a metaphor for a challenge or test. On your world, poisonous serpents can give you an initiation, such as when you survive a serpent's bite. Once bitten, you must transcend the poison through your consciousness or die. That is a dramatic example, and there are no poison-serpent tests in this school.

The nine serpents have more to do with the nine traps of the ego — or of physicality — that can keep you from awakening. When you first come in to physical life from a more expansive realm, the experience of physicality is very intense. The One wanted to experience this separation, even if it didn't really know what that meant. It didn't know how intense and, frankly, weird, a life of separation could be. So what happens?

Consciousness incarnates into a body and is overwhelmed by the challenge of physicality. To process this, humans most often shut down because the experience is just too intense. This is a third-density experience, which we explained in an earlier chapter. This is where humanity has been for approximately 13,000 years. As a species, you are now beginning to transition into fourth density, which is when you start releasing the experience of separation and begin integrating what you previously held as separate. You begin remembering who you really are.

The challenge of going from the One to this painful, separated experience can seem insurmountable. The School of the Nine Serpents was a way to begin awakening amid the challenges of being physical. Let us give you a metaphor: Imagine a net or a cloth with interwoven threads. Nets can be tightly woven or loosely woven. In third-density reality, the net is woven very tightly. This is the net of illusion. Your sense of separation, even though an illusion, is very tightly woven. There is no space, and you feel trapped. You become lost in the illusion.

When you start to awaken, it's as if the net loosens, and you sense spaces in the weave. Those spaces are like doorways or portals in which you can glimpse your true nature. At that point, you begin having spiritual experiences that perhaps connect you with the One. These experiences might last only a moment, but sometimes a moment is enough. Once you have a glimmer of your greater self, it is hard to close your eyes again.

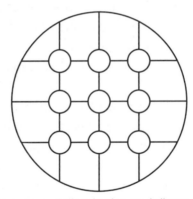

Figure 5.2. This image symbolizes the nine ego challenges to awakening.

Taking the metaphor further, imagine a zoomed-in version of a net, with nine crossing points where the threads intersect. [See figure 5.2.] These nine points symbolically represent nine serpents, much like nine gates through which you must pass. These nine serpents represent nine ego challenges to awakening. Each of these ego challenges has its own school, hence the School of the Nine Serpents.

We mentioned that this work is multi-incarnational, so many going through this training would incarnate and work only in one school in a lifetime. Remember, we also said that some of these old priests and priestesses who were part ET had very long life spans. These human/ET hybrids who were trained as the first priests and priestesses spent thousands of years — spanning many lifetimes — training through these nine schools. True evolution requires patience!

The Nine Schools of Awakening

In previous chapters we talked about the Golden Lake and the incarnational process. Whenever a drop has an experience in one of the nine schools, that experience is shared with the Lake, and subsequent drops benefit from that experience. (Remember that while we have to explain this in a linear way, the process isn't linear.) The nine schools are

1. School of Thought
2. School of Emotion
3. School of Pain
4. School of Pleasure
5. School of Elements and Sensations
6. School of Personality and Identity
7. School of Addiction/Attachment/Craving
8. School of Projection and Resistance (Advanced)
9. School of Integration (Advanced)

Consider each school as one of the crossing points on the metaphorical net we discussed. Each time you master one of the schools, the net loosens. The more schools you master, the looser the net becomes. The awakening process speeds up exponentially as you see and embrace the bigger picture that was once forgotten by your separated self.

Even as the net loosens, challenges arise. If a metaphorical hole in the net gets big, your ego might rationalize that you don't need to train in the pain school, for example. You might try to slip through the net without completing the process. But if you try to evade a training, it's as if the threads of the net shrink energetically and hold you in illusion once again. This is how the awakening process works: The more progress you make, the more intense the next challenge becomes. In the end, there is no way out except through.

Let us look briefly at what these schools mean. It is tempting to think they are sequential or linear, but that is not the case. The holographic principle applies here.

1. School of Thought. This school trains you how to differentiate between what is true consciousness and what is only thought generated by the human mind. As a human in separated reality, you tend to believe your thoughts to such an extent that you do not relinquish them even when they cause pain. This is usually the first step, because without doing this work, you cannot loosen the net of illusion any further. This school teaches you the difference between thought and consciousness.

2. School of Emotion. In this school, you learn how to use emotion as a tool and to not be a slave to emotion. The school teaches you how to fully embrace emotion in an integrated way so that it flows through you instead of being trapped inside. The idea sounds easy, but thoughts and emotions are strong forces that can easily trap you in the net. Since humans have a Vegan lineage, you have a strong tendency to repress emotion. This school teaches you how to use your emotion as a flow of energy instead of repressing or controlling it.

3. School of Pain. As a physical being, pain — whether mental, emotional, physical, or spiritual pain — is inevitable. This school helps you learn the difference between nondual pain and suffering, which is more polarized. Let us define this. Anyone in a physical body feels pain. When you feel pain from a neutral place, it is merely a sensation you can release or integrate. If you do not deny or attach to the pain, it moves through you. Suffering has to do with attachments you make to the pain, such as hatred of pain, avoidance of it, or any rejection arising in your reality. This school is extremely powerful, and it is one of the main juncture points on the net. When you master pain, you experience an indescribable level of freedom that creates a momentum that accelerates your awakening.

4. School of Pleasure. Many initiates look forward to this school but do not realize how difficult it is. This school deals with a specific attachment to pleasure. Pleasure is the opposite of pain. You avoid pain and crave pleasure. Pleasure is a challenging trap, because when you experience pleasure, you crave more; life becomes a quest for pleasure. This is not saying that pleasure is bad. The school trains you to experience pleasure 100 percent in the moment and then let it go. It trains you to not chase it. In a sense, this school is very sneaky, because you have to be very self-aware of your personal tendencies. There are other, subtler teachings included in this school as well.

5. School of Elements and Sensations. This school has to do with embracing physicality as a path to awakening. We mentioned how new souls can feel overwhelmed when they incarnate as humans. How do you navigate this? How do you fully embody yourself on Earth? This is a paradox, because the One wanted to experience separation, but the separated part screams, "No! I don't want to be here!" The prime directive of the One is to experience separation, but as a separated being, you resist. You develop coping mechanisms, ways to deny emotion. You avoid physical pain. The mind pulls you into a constant loop of dialog. Consequentially, most humans never fully incarnate in third density and thus experience a lot of suffering. You don't really fully embody yourself until fourth density.

Your beautiful Sirian Galactic Family saw your pain and discomfort as you rejected full embodiment and thus stayed stuck. This school teaches you ways to use the elements of physicality to help you embody and adjust to the Earth plane and release the resistance to do so. It is meant to bring ease, stability, and balance to physical beings. But here is another paradox: You can never fully be free of the net until you fully embrace physicality. You have to go deep into the experience of separation to be free of it. The only way out is in.

6. School of Personality and Identity (the Ego Teachings). This school trains you to go beyond seeing yourself as a personality or an identity. It helps you shift your perspective away from ego identity and more toward the One. It also teaches you how to use a personality and identity and how to "wear a human suit" when needed and when to put it aside. It also trains you to not get trapped in identity, and it reminds you of the true nature of the ego.

7. School of Addiction, Attachment, and Craving. This is often the hardest school to transcend, and students spent a lot of time here. Once you come into physicality and experience the chaos of physical sensation, you look for something to bring comfort. We are not just talking about alcohol or sex, for example. Thought patterns can be addictive, which is a form of delusional thinking that keeps you from feeling pain. This school is very deep — almost like a maze. Many get stuck here. But just like the School of Pain (3), when you navigate through it and release the juncture point on the net, you experience a huge shift in consciousness.

8. School of Projection and Resistance. This was an advanced school instructors introduced once the student had made progress through the other schools. It is advanced because it requires you to embrace the truth of the reflective universe, meaning you accept that whatever you see outside you is always a reflection of you. Understanding this experientially and with the mind can dramatically shift your consciousness, but it requires a lot of self-honesty and self-perception. We include the concept of resistance here, because the school includes working with your resistance to accepting the idea of the reflective universe. This truth is not one that the ego willingly embraces.

9. School of Integration. This is the last school and the only one in a fixed order; you work in this school when you have mastered all

92
Calling Our Parts Home

Sirius
FUTURE

the others. You can call it graduate work, if you like. Card 92 of the *Galactic Heritage Cards* is called Calling Our Parts Home. That is the card of integration, and its energy is similar to the School of Integration. Sirians were masters of integration training and have much wisdom to offer in this regard.

For now, we will work more with the School of Elements and Sensation (5), and your ability to root your attention on the sensation of those elements as a way to, in a sense, loosen one of the junctures of the net. If you are familiar at all with Lyssa and I, you can see that over many years, we've given you bits and pieces from these schools. Now we are accelerating the information.

From Separation to Integration

We would like to dialog with you even though you may be still digesting this material. Do you have any questions?

In a past retreat, Hamón [the Sirian] led a meditation in which we jumped into the

Golden Lake and jumped into the pain, so to speak. I went through this unbelievable pain in real life after that, and it has continued for over a year now. I've learned about and experienced pain and how to get out of it. I have also asked you, Sasha, about why these things are happening to me. You explained that my soul wanted to experience pain and changed a timeline to experience that. Consciously, I was not aware of making such a choice.

Correct, because the ego does not make the choice.

You then talked about the nine schools and the School of Pain (3), and about how intense and challenging it was. Although I am not consciously attending that school right now, I feel at my soul level I have been going to that school for the past year. If my soul has been in the School of Pain in the past and all time is simultaneous, then the current and past experiences exist together. Maybe in this life I am actually acting out or experiencing what I didn't learn in this past year.

Yes, you have the opportunity to finish the School of Pain (3). But guess what? To finish it means you have to experience pain, right? "Finishing" is a charged word. It has expectation attached to it. The ego wants to know when the end is. But finishing is an unknown, and the process is not linear. To "graduate" from this school, you learn to embrace pain fully — without polarized preference or resistance — and embrace it as a tool for further growth. Now you can see why this is one of the least popular schools!

I don't know much about the transition from third to fourth density. Does it mean that humans right now are more receptive to this kind of information?

Yes, because you are moving into a cycle of integration. You are not as separated, and there is less polarization. Earlier we made the comment that as you move into fourth density, you embody yourself more. Let us clarify. In third density, you come into a realm of separation. It is intense, chaotic, and the ego resists it. You push away pain and chase pleasure. But as you move into fourth density, one of the characteristics of integration is that you stop resisting things like pain. You stop resisting things you don't like. You stop trying to control. Instead, you embrace the entire experience of physicality, and that is what we mean by embodying yourself more. You become more present. We realize this is a paradox: When you become fully present in fourth density, it means you have surrendered to your experience of physicality. Then it is time to go Home.

For those of you familiar with Zen, you have heard Zen masters say, "If you are washing the dishes, then just wash the dishes." Your mind should not be doing something else. You need to be fully embodied in the sensation of the soap and water. When the mind is not "out there" but with the body and when the emotions are not "out there" but feeling the experience of the moment, you become an integrated being.

This is why the first school, the School of Thought (1), is so important. In third density, thought rules. As simplistic as it sounds, as you move into fourth density, thought no longer rules. Sensation rules. We are not talking about the sensation of pain or things that pull you away from your center. We are talking about the sensation that Zen masters describe, which is being fully present with everything that arises in every moment. You root your experience of physicality in the now. This now, then this now, then this now, and so on. This leads to awakening.

You've talked about the School of the Nine Serpents. I feel a strong connection to Sirius and that my soul comes from there. So what am I still doing here after all this time? I'm still here and haven't graduated. I feel like a dropout! I realize my sense of time is still linear, but is there still something unfinished to do here?

This is the linear perspective, yes, but it is not the whole story. Do not feel badly for not understanding, because nonlinear concepts are hard to describe in words. Let us use an analogy by discussing the *Galactic Heritage Cards*, even if you are not familiar with them.

In the deck, the physical civilizations are referenced by using three eras of the species: past, present, and future. These refer to the evolutionary stages of a civilization. Imagine the deck as a representation of the journey into separation and back into wholeness. In the deck, you have first-era Sirius, which is the young species. Then you have second-era Sirius, which is a bit more mature and heading toward species adulthood, and then you have third-era Sirius, the awakened ones. All three eras exist simultaneously in the deck, just like you have counterparts in all eras.

So here you are in this life right now asking this question. This connects you to second-era Sirius, because that is the stage Earth is experiencing too. But there are other yous. You have counterparts in all eras and from many time streams. Your consciousness plays out the whole story, which is the holographic principle. But the you who is here in this room, with this ego, is a vital piece of the puzzle. Without the you in this room, the whole puzzle is incomplete. Therefore, you are not a dropout even though you might feel like one. Some version of you has to be in this room with this experience, or the tapestry is not complete.

The idea of time and parallel universes is hard to understand with only the mind. We have found that in working with humans, the only way people start to understand it is by having an experience of unlocking from time. These are quantum experiences where you feel yourself on all levels of creation simultaneously. This is why scientists have such a challenge with understanding quantum mechanics, because they try to understand it from a separated, left-brain perspective. Quantum states are pure consciousness. It is a vital part of the equation. It is only through experience that you can understand your quantum self.

I have the desire to evolve. Is this a human or universal desire?

Actually, it is a bit of both. Your big One self is like a magnet. Your natural state is integration. So the One you energetically pulls you toward integration. When you say you have a desire for evolution, part of you senses the flow. That is not based on the ego. When the ego gets involved, it says, "If I buy this tool, I can evolve." "If I do this workshop, I can evolve." When you try to control or speed your evolution or bypass necessary lessons, usually the ego is running the show. But when you just live your life and take every opportunity to evolve — even if it is observing a leaf on the sidewalk or having a painful experience — then life lives through you. It is a very different kind of experience. It is more of a fourth-density experience.

Another paradox is that evolution happens most when you let go. "But I don't want to let go!" That is the voice of third density. Many of the nine schools address this issue. Your ego wants to help you evolve. It might give you suggestions, and that is okay. Just allow yourself to accept life as the greatest teacher. When you do, you feel the tide of evolution move you back to the One.

How does this integrative process influence the growth of the soul? If a physical civilization is more integrated, how does that affect the growth of the soul?

They are entirely interconnected. It has to do with the holographic model of consciousness. If you look back at the model of the concentric circles, the outer cycle — which contains the smaller, separated circle — is representative of the One. The essence of the One is holographic. If you cut pieces of the One into tiny sections representing separate souls, every tiny piece still contains the complete pattern of creation within it. While a piece might experience the illusion of separation, its nature is still complete and whole. Thus, if evolution happens on the micro level, it also happens on the macro level. You cannot separate the process at all. Everything is connected.

The Cause of Pain

I want to return to the idea of pain. There are two kinds of pain: emotional and physical. With emotional pain, I feel that if we change our belief systems, then it is easy to release. In my case, I always have physical pain when something happens, which I know is resistance of some kind. But sometimes I can't bear the pain and want to delete it. But the only way to completely delete pain is to die. When you talked about being in a higher mental perspective to overcome pain, that is like a hard-core monk. I cannot do that. Can you give any advice to overcome this pain?

Well, this topic could be a whole book. For now, we will say there are two kinds of pain. The first is injury to the body, such as putting your hand in a fire, which is purely physical pain. Then there is emotional pain, which first reveals itself physically. Examples are migraines, back problems, unexplained fevers, digestive problems, and others. These come and go. Even though they manifest as physical pain, they are usually denied emotional pain. How do you deal with that?

This is one of the biggest lessons playing out on your world right now. So much emotional pain on Earth shows up as physical pain. People do not connect physical pain with emotional pain, so they take drugs. It numbs the physical condition, but the energy of the repressed emotion is still there. Even the symptoms can change. So what do you do?

If you were in a civilization deep in third density, this wouldn't be much of an issue. It is a huge issue on your world now, because you are transitioning. When you go through this type of transition, everything that was pushed down needs to come out. It will come out any way it can. The School of Pain (3) also deals with this issue of how to use pain to awaken yourself. Pain can be used as a doorway to the emotional body. But here is the challenge: The mind thinks, "If I'm going to do emotional processing, I should try to figure out what the issue is." That kind of approach does not release the charge, because you stay in the mental realm. This is often why traditional therapy doesn't always work. You have to release the charge somehow. When you meditate, allow yourself to go into your quantum state (your One self) and feel the pain there. When you do, the charge starts releasing. When you work with this regularly, you start to become aware of the cause, but it isn't always necessary to know. It is layered.

When we talk about layers, perhaps the first layer of the pain is something like, "My father didn't really love me." If you get to that layer, stay with the feeling and don't run from it. Don't analyze it. Don't invalidate it. Just sit with the pain and truly feel it. This is what we mean by embodying emotion. The charge starts releasing at this point, but then another layer might come up. This one might be a past-life situation that mirrors your present-life pain. Again, it is just another layer. Eventually, it might lead all the way back to what we call the original wound. This is something the mind cannot access because it makes no sense. It arises not as a thought but as a wave of emotion or energy.

Original wounds always mirror human wounds, but they are deeper and more primal and universal or archetypal. If the human wound is, "My father didn't love me," the mirrored original wound could be, "Creation doesn't love me; I was kicked out of heaven." Original wounds lead back to the pain of the original separation from the One. The mind and ego cannot understand this, but the soul does. You can think of it as ripples in the Golden Lake generated from an original action — a stone dropping into the water. The different waves represent the different ways the original wound reverberates through the Lake.

You can understand original wounds intellectually, but the charge doesn't release until you move experientially through the doorway to the pain. You first work on the human level, and then you go deeper, all the way back to the original wound. It isn't always linear, as we've described, so the ego has to relinquish control of the process and just follow the path of healing presented to you.

We know this sounds like monk's work. The ego will tell you, "I can't do that; it is monk's work." The ego says these things to stop you from destroying the illusion. To be blunt, at this point of evolution, humanity doesn't have a choice whether they do this work or not. No civilization can avoid it. Like toothpaste in a tube with the cap on, the tube will burst if you put too much pressure on it. This is the energy humans carry now and why you have so many mental-health crises. Humans have to take the metaphorical cap off the tube and allow all that trapped energy to release. Please don't be afraid, because you all move at the pace that is right for you.

We have shared a lot of information. Please know you don't have to understand it all 100 percent. The information itself triggers and unlocks memories within you. Actually, it isn't just memories; you can say energy packets are triggered. The Sirians left packets of energy and light within human DNA in the ancient days. As evolutionary energy gets to a certain point, these packets are triggered. This is already happening. When we transmit information such as this, more of these energy packets are unpacked. The ego thinks it needs to understand, as if it is just intellectual information, but understanding is not really necessary.

Reflections

As I was learning about the School of the Nine Serpents, I realized that everyone on Earth is feeling anxiety or pain. Sometimes it seems that we are on the verge of war. What can we, as individuals, do to navigate this?

This goes back to the School of Projection and Resistance (8), the advanced school. It has to do with the lesson that everything external is a reflection of the internal. The craziness you see in the world does not happen independently from what happens inside you. It is a reflection of what happens inside you. Thus, the anxiety everyone feels is not because of external events. External events happen because of unrecognized, unprocessed, internal pain. You asked what you can do. There is really only one thing you can do: Go inward. Go inward and meet the demons there. Meet the things you don't want to see. Take ownership of the reality you've created. Ownership, a negative polarity, is not blame.

The School of Addiction, Attachment, and Craving (7) shows you that one of the most insidious addictions is focusing on the external as a way to avoid the internal. That is one of the most significant addictions you must break, and it is one of the most challenging to heal.

The truth is that looking over here is a reflection. Looking over there is a reflection. Reality is a mirror, and you must accept and understand this truth on more than an intellectual level. When you do accept it, your internal work moves to a much deeper level. This is why the School of Projection and Resistance (8) is an advanced school. It is like learning to navigate a mirror room at an amusement park. Distortion is everywhere except when you sincerely look within.

That might be an esoteric answer to your question, and you might still wonder if there is something else you can do. Many of you, especially Lyssa's channeling students, have already started this work. It requires you to look at the pains and unrecognized emotions that lie deep in your unconscious and learn to understand them in a nonintellectual way. Feel them, then release them. When you really go into those places and allow yourself to see what you don't want to see, and then rest there with the emotion, the release process starts.

Working with your emotions in this way is part of the School of Elements and Sensations (5). Working with your breath and emotions helps you root your awareness in the sensation of the emotion, thus encouraging the full embodiment we referred to earlier.

If you are not actively in touch with the flow of your emotions, you feel emotions in your body. When you have a pain in your neck, you believe you slept wrong, and a pain pill or massage will fix it. This is part of the addiction to projecting externally what really happens internally. Yes, sometimes you might sleep in a weird position. But if the pain is chronic, it is usually repressed emotional pain. You can use that sensation of pain as a doorway to unlock the emotional body. This is very profound training, and it can lead to your freedom as a spiritual being.

This wisdom cannot be forced. Most deeper spiritual teachings seem hidden. They only come to you when you really need them and when you are ready. If you are not ready, what use are they? Those of you asking questions and doing this work have another important role. You are, in a sense, starting this deep inner work for others. You are making it easier for others to do this work when they are ready.

To summarize, when you see chaos in the world, resist the

addiction of believing it comes from "out there," and look inside. Find the pain in you those outside things triggered. That is where the work begins.

In regard to the leaders of our world, most are very far away from wanting to look at themselves. From an ET point of view, why do you think these people are in leadership positions?

These unbalanced leaders are the externalization of things inside that you have collectively denied. If a whole planet does their inner work, the planet does not have to create leaders to play out these archetypal issues. With these leaders, you see the addiction to control and egos in tremendous pain, mostly on the inner-child level. That inner child acts out in pain. These people are macrocosmic reflections of what happens on the microcosmic level. This kind of thing happens on nearly every planet at this point in its evolution. Most planets, in their third-density phase, have denied parts of themselves. So when these personalities emerge on the world stage, they get you to look at yourself. The key is to look at yourself without judgment and with supreme compassion for the part that is in pain. Looking at yourself and your pain with the deepest love and compassion shifts the whole dynamic.

Are you saying that if we all start looking within at our pain that maybe we can change the world?

Absolutely, yes. We know the mind translates and distorts communication, so we are really picky about our words. Egos can never change the world. As you look at yourself and experience these inner transformations, your perception of the world automatically changes because it is a reflection of you.

In the past, you have talked about the dark time in Orion that is already healed. I want to know what kind of energy is healed Orion energy? How did that healing take place?

As you know, the Orion civilization was deeply polarized in its past. When opposite sides try to change or control the other, they get deadlocked. There can be no movement. Through thousands of years, that dynamic could not shift. How do you transform that kind of energy?

We were just talking about the connection between internal and external realities. Each side of the Orion energy viewed the other as something that had to be changed or controlled. The other side was always blamed. They did not look within or take ownership of the reality they had created. At one point, the pressure became too much. One subgroup within the Orion system began doing the inner work. For those of you who know your Orion history, this group has been labeled the Black League. These were the freedom fighters. They were also the spiritual priests. They began to have revelations that come at certain points in evolution about the connection between inner and outer realities. If two sides are locked in an energetic dance, how do you change the dance? One partner changes the steps, and the whole dance has to change.

A martial art called Aikido works with energy flow. You don't meet force with force; you meet force with flow so that the one using force gets that force reflected back to them. As the Black League began working inwardly, the whole dynamic changed, and they began to integrate. They were not capable of dancing the old dance anymore, so both sides had to change.

Germane refers to three eras of the Orion civilization in the *Galactic Heritage Cards*. The past, or first era, was the darkest, most polarized time. The second era, the present, was when transformation and healing began. The third era, the future, was what naturally happened from that integration: awakening. Within your galactic family, the Orion energy is seen as the epitome of polarity integration. The last four cards of the deck express that necessary reintegration before returning to the One.

Even though you are here on Earth and the Orion drama has long since completed in linear time, the energy of the complete hologram of creation still remains. Those of you still processing polarity and control dramas can hook into old Orion energy, which can help you bring up issues that still need healing. This is one reason you still see Orion energy playing out on the collective Earth level. It isn't because the evil Orion empire is controlling you. It is because old Orion energy serves as a trigger to help you all heal your inner polarity. Once again, the external is a reflection of the internal. The entire energy dynamic of your experience in separation is encoded in the hologram, and you can tap into it whenever you need to learn your lessons.

The Role of the Ego

What is the role of the ego in the School of Elements and Sensations (5)?

Ego can help or hinder the awakening process. You can think of the ego as a filter that acts as a translation device between your human and spiritual selves. But first, let us define our view of the ego, because many people think of it in a negative way.

If your true state of consciousness is the One and you want to experience separation, how do you do that? It is very difficult. It is like trying to tie a helium balloon to the ground, which is a metaphor for how consciousness naturally awakens. Consciousness needs a mechanism to help it fragment in order to experience separation so that it can be grounded here in physical reality. The ego is a neutral mechanism that performs that function. Processing the experience of separation and relaying that experience back to the One is an important job.

As a human being, sensation is one of the most important ways you receive the experience of separation. Pain and pleasure are examples. One of the school's trainings is experiencing sensation in a purely neutral way with no story attached.

We do a group exercise where we poke participants in their feet with a rock. This roots attention to the feet and is an opportunity to retrain the ego how to do its most basic job — the reason for its existence — which is to experience separation and sensation neutrally without a story. As you go deeper and deeper into the experience of separation, you lose the capability to be neutral. You go deeper into illusion, with the ego creating stories to protect itself from pain. This is the point where the ego's essential neutral job distorts and gets lost in illusion. The process of awakening is the journey back from illusion — back to the essential neutral job of the ego in a physical body.

You come from spirit into physical reality. The ego is a mechanism to help you organize reality in a neutral way. It helps you process sensation as a separate being. But eventually you fall further into sleep and experience the deepest illusion in separation. On the way back to awakening, you retrace your steps and go back the way you came, to the point of neutrality. [This was outlined in chapter 1, in the diagram called Layers of Experience. This material is also part of the School of the Nine Serpents.]

Third-density experience is the fall into illusion. As you move into fourth density and the awakening process starts, you gradually move back to the neutral function of the ego. As Pleiadians in fourth density, we still have egos, because we still have bodies. But our egos have that neutral function in which they purely serve as a way to perceive and experience life without stories in a realm of separation. We've returned to the essential neutral nature of what ego was meant to be. You are now making that journey back to the neutral expression of ego. One of the training methods to help you make this transition is using sensation.

How do you use sensation to do this? Most of you know the basic idea of what sensation is in terms of the body, but there is also emotional sensation. If you have intense grief, focus on the grief instead of running from it. Let yourself feel. If you surrender and stay neutral, the feeling transforms. Some yoga practices now teach this philosophy. When you are in a posture, wise teachers will tell you to bring the mind to the breath and feel the sensation of the pose without trying to evade its discomfort. They might tell you the same thing if emotions come up in a pose. Stay with it, and don't run. The yoga boom is perfectly timed, because these are the types of trainings you need to help bring the ego back to its neutral function.

If you can stay present with all sensations and not run from them, what happens? When done repeatedly, it creates a powerful alchemy within you — not only on the yoga mat but also in life. Your consciousness expands, and you go through the doorway of pain and begin releasing what has been repressed. This type of training is part of the School of Elements and Sensations (5).

The Higher Heart

As you move more deeply into fourth density, a new energy center activates. This energy center is in the area of the thymus, above the heart. It has a combined energy of both the heart and throat chakras, and it allows you to embody more love, utilizing more refined heart energy. When we say "embody more love," we don't mean the human kind of love. We are talking about universal love: You embody more of the true self, or the One consciousness. We use the word "love" because, from a human point of view, you will feel more love.

We know that many of you have had this experience. Perhaps it lasts a minute, an hour, or if you are super lucky, a day. You feel much love and beauty in the universe for no reason. In that moment, you feel as if that connection has no obstacles. Imagine feeling that for your whole life. This is a fourth-density experience that gets more and more profound as you move deeper through the fourth-density spectrum.

When you live from that fourth-density place, the ego begins expressing its primary purpose — to help you feel what it is like to be separate with no story or judgment. What does sensation feel like in that place? It is magnified. Your heart cannot contain the beauty of the sun, of nature, because it is so great. Maybe you feel pain and pleasure together. You welcome that paradox. Maybe the taste of tea is magnified to the point of ecstasy. The love you feel toward a child who is a stranger to you expands your heart.

The point we are making is that sensation at that level is supermagnified. If this were to happen to you in third density, it would be too intense to process. You have a condition on your world called autism. People with autism are very sensitive. It is hard for them to live in the world when they feel sensation that strongly. They represent this new capacity we are talking about. This is the early emergence of it. They are the pioneers, in a sense, breaking through the old paradigm of a third-density collective that doesn't want to feel. Caregivers of those who are autistic have to learn how this person sees the world. That knowledge and compassion enters mass consciousness.

This higher heart center, the thymus, is awakening from a long sleep. This is another reason why the teachings of the School of Elements and Sensations (5) are so important now. As you go deeper into fourth density, you will have a much greater capacity for feeling sensation. Getting to that place from where you are now requires traveling a road where you have to open yourself more and more. When you open yourself more and allow yourself to go into deep and open vulnerability, pain often arises. Humans don't like to feel pain; thus, you close up.

Right now, an open-closed dual energy is happening, which can make you feel as if you're being pulled in many directions. You experience great openness and sometimes great closure. It will not always be like this. This is part of the adjustment process for developing the higher heart center; it helps you increase your capacity to process sensations in the physical world.

Sensation Homework

We wish to give you some homework. For this homework, we ask you to work with sensation in a much more focused way. Practice bringing your complete attention to whatever sensation you are experiencing instead of always going into your mind. The point is to immerse yourself in the sensation so that nothing else exists.

When you are in the bath, how does the water feel? We are not talking about mentally making a list of what you are feeling, because that is a mental exercise. Instead, melt into the experience itself. Let your body surrender to the water of the bath, feeling what it is like without commentary. You will be surprised how much your mind narrates the experience. If it does, don't worry; let it go and return to the sensation.

How can you practice this in daily life? Let's say you are on a bus, and someone is wearing really strong, pungent perfume. You can tolerate the odor or get mad, but can you relax into it instead? Again, it is like relaxing into an uncomfortable yoga pose. There might be resistance. Try to be with it neutrally without commentary. Unpleasant things are harder to work with than pleasant ones, but both trainings are necessary. This is your homework if you choose to embrace it. Watch where repeated practice of this homework takes you in your consciousness. Over time, you will notice shifts.

The School of Personality and Identity (6)
LESSON: SERVICE TO SELF VERSUS SERVICE TO OTHERS

We would like to focus on a teaching from the sixth school. This is the school that contains teachings about the ego. We wish to talk about this because your planet is in a lot of pain right now. As we've said, this is common when you shift from third to fourth density. We'd like you to become aware of a specific dynamic that is connected to your ego. As with most dynamics of the ego, there is duality.

This dynamic has to do with service to self versus service to others. Humanity struggles mightily with this, and in speaking with many of you, we know you struggle with it as well. It is easy to think that service to self and service to others represent opposite energy. There is a belief that you either serve yourself or you serve others, but subtle dynamics are at play here. Instead of opposites, there is a spectrum of experience on both sides of the coin, so to speak.

First, let us look at the spectrum for service to others, which you can see in table 5.1. On the left end (#1) is the pole of sacrifice. This represents those who sacrifice their souls or lives for others. People often do this for loved ones. But this pole on the left represents a type of sacrifice that most humans don't do, and as noble as it sounds, it is not healthy for normal human beings. The few beings at the far end of this spectrum are either fully awakened, such as masters, or robots.

Now look at the other end of the spectrum (#2). This represents giving service but withholding your true self. It is inauthentic. Perhaps you do it to look good or to receive some kind of acknowledgement. When you give inauthentic service, resentment builds in your unconscious mind until it bubbles over to your conscious mind. Neither end of the spectrum seems very fun, right? On one end, you sacrifice who you are. On the other end, you are just faking it and not truly giving anything of yourself.

With any spectrum, there is a middle point, which is marked in the diagram. The middle point represents where you authentically give service but don't sacrifice yourself. It is a very thin line on which to stand, but it is a point of stillness and balance. You can easily fall off that line, yes? Life in polarized reality is challenging, and this is a challenge for the ego. How can you be authentic and at the same time not give your soul away, so to speak?

Now let us look at the other side of the coin: service to self. This can also be an interesting and painful experience. On one end of the

SERVICE TO OTHERS	SERVICE TO SELF
☯	☯
Spectrum 1<————|————>2	Spectrum 3<————|————>4
Left End: Sacrifice Right End: Inauthentic Service/Resentment	3 Left End: Denial/Rejection 4 Right End: Indulgence

Table 5.1. Range of service indicates level of awakening.

spectrum, you have indulgence. You have the mythical god Narcissus, who embodies this archetypal idea. Then you have the other end of the spectrum, which is denial or rejection of the self. This pattern often forms when you are abused as a child and you believe you are not worthy of love. Most people are not at this far end of the spectrum. There is also a middle point on this spectrum. The middle point is experiencing self-love that is not indulgent and is fully balanced, without guilt.

What phase of evolution is Earth in now? Two of the strongest energies playing out on Earth are those of indulgence and sacrifice. You will find that people in the most pain are those who are not in balance on the spectrum; they experience too much self-sacrifice or too much ego indulgence.

You might be wondering how too much indulgence can be painful. This is because you can be so out of balance that self-indulgence is the only way you can deal with the pain. It is as if you contain a black hole. You try to get love and energy, but the only method you know is to grab them from others and try to give to them to yourself. If you look at people like psychopaths, cult leaders, and maybe even some politicians, their actions are the result of their cravings to fill their emptiness. This creates massive inner pain.

Deep self-sacrifice comes from a refusal or inability to accept that you are worthy of love and respect. The origins of this pattern can come from very dark places associated with abuse. These are the dramatic ends of the spectrum that do not represent the majority of humanity, but it helps you understand the dynamic. You need to understand these dynamics to see aspects of them within yourself. The teachings of the School of the Nine Serpents assists you to move to the center point of balance and come to a place of peace within.

You might be thinking: "Philosophies are nice, but how do I apply this in my life? How do I use this knowledge to awaken?" Being aware of the dynamic is the first step. If you are not a psychopath or a cult leader, then the biggest challenge is usually self-sacrifice. If you choose to accept our advice, then we suggest you watch yourself from a neutral and nonjudgmental place. How much do you sacrifice your true self, and what is really an acceptable level?

One of the reasons these teachings are so deep is that the ego can continue to deceive you as you do the inner work. Continued deeper work that takes you through layers, when done properly, can keep you one step ahead of the ego. Remember that the ego doesn't have to fix anything and is actually incapable of doing so. What is more important is cultivating the ability to see your patterns clearly and honestly and then letting yourself feel the emotional pain. Be present with what is there without trying to change or erase it. Feel deeply, without distortion or judgment.

When you train yourself to do that, you will see amazing changes unfold in your life. Remember that with this process, the ego doesn't do anything. This is one reason the path of awakening taught by this school can take many lifetimes. The ego tries to jump in and save the day, all while convincing you it isn't really ego. It doesn't work that way.

A Road Map Home

I know there are many kinds of lessons my soul can learn. How can I know when I am in the right place at the right time in any given circumstance?

This is a wonderful question. It is impossible for you to ever be in the wrong place at the wrong time. The universe makes no mistakes. The ego sometimes asks this question when it really wants to ask, "How can I only be in the place I always want to be?" There is a misunderstanding that when something good happens, you are in the right place, and when something bad happens, you are in the wrong place. That is only ego perception. You can never be in the wrong place. Even when you are in a place of indecision, that place of indecision is the right place, because you might need that rest period between actions. The ego cannot ever control things. One of the symptoms of your ongoing awakening process is when you perceive and accept that you are always where you need to be in every moment and relax with that truth.

Let's say you walk down the street and a man on a bicycle is texting. The bicycle hits you, and you break your leg. If we continue with the premise that it is impossible to be in the wrong place at the wrong time, it means this event was necessary for you. It was part of the flow of the universe for a reason that you might never know. If you deny the event or judge yourself or if you blame the man on the bicycle, then you suffer even more. When you are not fully present with your experiences, you suffer.

Going back to the School of the Nine Serpents, was it only present in Japan? What about Hong Kong and other areas in the world?

In the ancient days, these schools were present in many areas. The schools in the West were a little different from those in the East, but they were very connected. In Japan, several very large centers had schools in the ancient days. One large area was around Lake Towada in northern Japan. Smaller schools were in the areas of Tenkawa shrine and the mountains around Kyoto, including Lake Biwa. Many schools were located in areas of the south, including Okinawa, Hong Kong, Thailand, and even as far south as Bali. The West had too many schools to count in South America, Central America, and North America. The same is true for the other continents on your world. Because we speak to many of you who live in Asia, we often focus on the Asian schools.

As a side note, the Okinawan islands are referred to as the Ryukyu Kingdom. While there might be differences in Kanji, many of you know that "ryu" means dragon and "kyu" means nine, thus nine dragons/serpents. This school was known in very ancient days by that name, especially in the East.

In the end, do we graduate from the School of the Nine Serpents?

These teachings were given in much depth in the ancient days, and they were like planting seeds within your mass consciousness. The seeds laid dormant as your evolutionary cycle went more deeply into forgetfulness and separation, which is normal for planetary development. As you enter more active evolutionary cycles, the seeds are stimulated to sprout. The core of your galaxy is like a metronome, managing the evolutionary pace of its planets. As humanity begins this new evolutionary cycle, the energy from the galactic core guides the entire process.

Those of you attracted to these teachings have experienced them before, and you are continuing your training. It is not a formal school, per se. You won't get a certificate. But for those of you continuing your training from other lives, the school reminds you of the framework of those ancient teachings and helps you grow. What is the result when it seems the teachings go to deeper and deeper levels? Ultimately, full awakening. But the work of awakening is a paradox, because you do not get a guarantee that you will awaken within fifty years, let's say.

The awakening process happens paradoxically when your ego gives up trying to control the awakening process. It is never a mentally guided experience. The School of the Nine Serpents helps your ego begin to let go of its addictive need to control. As you work on deeper and deeper levels of the school, you see the work has very little to do with doing anything. Instead, it has more to do with undoing (the ego) and relaxing into your true nature. Your true nature is already awakened and always has been.

The school helps you unlock from the perception of separation. It helps you remember who you are, beyond ego identity. The school doesn't teach you anything you don't already know deep within, but it helps you remember. It is like a map that leads you home. When you fully remember, you no longer need the map.

SIX

Ancient Pleiadians and the Golden Lake Teachings

SASHA AND AMA

S asha: This transmission was given at Lake Biwa near Kyoto, Japan. It is one of the oldest Lakes in the world and shares much history with your ancient Galactic Family. We present the following experiential exercise and meditation to help you tangibly feel the Golden Lake teachings. We know it is hard to meditate while reading text, so we suggest that you record the meditation in your voice and then listen to the recording or just imagine the journey as if you are reading a very engaging novel.

GOLDEN LAKE MEDITATION, PART 1
- Please take a moment to quiet yourself by imagining the gentle sound of water against a shore. Now bring your awareness to the calm Lake water itself. Imagine, for a moment, the sun rising over this Lake. As it rises, the water of the Lake turns golden. This Golden Lake represents your One consciousness.

There is only one One consciousness. Although you sit here in a physical body, the Lake is your original Home. It attracts the water in your cells like a magnet, pulling your consciousness toward it. Allow your consciousness to merge into the Golden Lake.

- As you merge with the Golden Lake, your consciousness melts into the water. Any resistance you have is released. Your physical body relaxes. Your mind relaxes. Your heart relaxes. You are aware of your body sitting on the shore, but you are simultaneously aware of your consciousness melting in the Lake. You are the small you and the Big You simultaneously. The cells of your physical body resonate with the frequency of the Golden Lake. The small self is always attracted to Home.

- Bring your attention to your heart space. If you sense really closely, you can sense your heart space has an inflow of energy. It comes from the consciousness of the Golden Lake. Breathe that energy into your heart on the in-breath. On the out-breath, let go of any resistance, pain, or contraction. Let it go.

- You might sense a gentle movement, like a wave or a flow. Let yourself ride that wave. Relax into it. As you relax, notice that the Lake stretches into infinity. It is limitless. There is no boundary. Take some quiet time here to feel the movement and flow of the Lake. This is the One consciousness that you are. Please pause and enjoy this experience as long as you wish.

- In this journey, it is night now. A beautiful clear sky full of stars appears above you. The Lake is still golden, and it reflects all stars. You are still the Lake, feeling the energy of the universe reflected in you. You are still the consciousness of the Lake, but you also sense another human aspect of you sitting on the shore in the distance. A drop from this Lake is attracted to this little human on the shore. That drop begins moving toward the human. It merges with the water in the cells of the human. As it does, it brings the memory and experience of the entire Lake with it. The hologram of creation from the Lake goes into your cells as the human sitting on the shore.

- Let yourself absorb this. While absorbing this, you realize you contain all that the Lake has experienced. The Lake holds everything experienced by every person on the shore. Every experience is within you too. This is how you are both the small self and the Big Self.
- Just allow yourself to rest in this place in your consciousness. As you rest, we will speak to you of ancient history.

Tens of thousands of years ago, my ancestors sat on the shores of this Lake with many early humans. We talked about the Golden Lake as a metaphor for your true self. This was the essence of the teachings we gave at the very beginnings of humanity, because it is always necessary for a species to know where they come from. When we say "come from," we do not mean from another star system; we mean your true Home as the One consciousness. You can call this place the Golden Lake or whatever you wish, as long as you remember its nature. This awareness is the key to all awakening.

Though my Pleiadian ancestors knew that humanity would take the journey through third density and deep separation, these teachings were given to plant seeds. Those seeds have lain dormant, but there have been times when they've spouted. In the cycle of evolution of your species, it is now time for the full sprouting. We are tying these two periods together: the ancient past when these ancient teachings were given for the first time and the present time that represents a pivotal point for humanity.

Collectively, you are moving into a confusing period of deep emotional release, which is a necessary part of a species awakening process. As you collectively move into that confusing emotional energy in order to release it, they can lose their way. But if you remember the teachings of the Golden Lake, you will never be lost. This is the guiding light.

We have said that deep concepts sometimes have to be communicated through metaphor, but metaphor can also dissolve blockages in the emotional body. When you tune in to this Golden Lake, feel its pull, and feel the "you" in the Lake, your heart frequency shifts. When your heart frequency shifts, blockages in your emotional body begin to melt like candle wax.

Together with the Sirian teachings of utilizing sensation to be fully present in the moment, we offer you these tools to assist in your awakening process.

Ancient Earth Teachings

In very ancient times, extraterrestrials (ETs) from older civilizations had a sacred responsibility to nurture younger civilizations. We also had to be very careful not to interfere. Thus, the work an ET civilization does with a new species trains the ET group as well. These ETs had to learn to do their work without interfering.

In those ancient days, various ET groups worked with new humans. The groups were all over the world. For this discussion, we will talk about one ancient Pleiadian group you might call elders. They would travel your world to human communities being guided by ET groups, and they would give specific teachings. Their responsibility was to help new humans remember their roots. When we say "roots," we do not mean only stars. We mean your roots all the way back to the One. Thus, the role of these Pleiadian elders was to help you remember the One consciousness that you are. These were the origins of the Golden Lake teachings.

Looking back to ancient times, a great many of these communities were found around lakes. Lakes represent a very stable resource. Also, the energy around lakes is very special; it is feminine, with qualities of receptivity and fluidity and the ability to go deep within the heart.

Lake Biwa, Japan, is at least 2 million years old. There is another area in northern Japan in the Aomori area called Lake Towada, which also had human communities guided by your Galactic Family. Other famous lakes on your world that had similar functions were Lake Titicaca in Peru and Bolivia, the Great Lakes region of the United States, and the great lake of Baikal in Siberia. These are just some examples.

Many myths about these lakes refer to them as birthplaces. Some myths even say they are the birthplaces of humanity. You can say that in a sense, the spirit of humanity was born in these places.

We wish to introduce this ancient group of Pleiadians to you. The channeled being, Ama, is known to several of Lyssa's channeling classes in Japan. She will give you further information.

Ama's Pleiadian Transmission

Ama: Greetings, my brothers and sisters. We are Ama. The concept of "I" versus "we" is confusing to us, so we will describe our orientation. Many tens of thousands of years ago, my group had physical bodies, much like Sasha does now. My group was responsible for working in many of these human communities that Sasha has just discussed. For us, this was a very, very long time ago. My species has since gone to the light. What do we mean by that? We no longer have bodies, and we no longer express the concept of "I." If you look at the metaphor of the Golden Lake, Ama is a drop from the Lake. We are also many drops. Many drops are Ama, and one drop is Ama. We understand this is confusing to humans. You can refer to me in the singular, but we are plural.

We are the group that was so active on your world a very long time ago. In a sense, you can say we've gone back to the Lake, and we continue the process of absorbing and becoming the full Lake. When we were here so long ago, the foundational teachings were simply called Teachings of the Lake. These teachings are alive once again on your world. You are receiving it at a much more sophisticated level than in ancient times. Sasha alluded to this a little earlier when she said you are at a critical point in your evolution. We return at these critical points to remind you of the Teachings of the Lake.

This transmission is about receiving. It is about deeply opening yourself and receiving these teachings purely on an energetic level. As you read these words, you open your channel to receive this energy transmission. You receive what is right for you.

This work has a higher purpose. It is to help you see and experience the many reflections of you within the Lake as representative of the living hologram that you are. As Sasha said, intellectual understanding is not enough any longer. Now you must bring the knowledge deep into yourself.

GOLDEN LAKE MEDITATION, PART 2

As with the previous meditation, you can record these words or read them in a relaxed way and allow your consciousness to journey with us as we guide you. Get in a comfortable position, and begin to relax your body and mind.

- Your mind drifts away like a boat on the Lake. Return to the feeling of being one with the Lake. Remember the feeling of that energy flowing to your heart. This creates what we call a torus field of energy around you. It comes in through the front of your chest, loops around out the back, and comes back in the front so that a continuous cycle is created. Your whole heart is open and flows in this way. You might eventually have the sensation of feeling expansion or pressure in your chest. If so, just relax and expand. As you expand, your sense of boundaries between your consciousness and the physical world becomes very thin. This process of expansion will continue throughout this exercise.

- Bring your attention to the cosmos, to where the Pleiades might be in the sky. It doesn't matter if you know its exact location; intention is key. See the Pleiades in your mind and feel it in your heart. With all this movement and inflow of energy into your heart, your heart is like a magnet. It pulls in an energy transmission from the Pleiades. This transmission is slightly different for each of you.

- Sasha has talked about the idea of a fractal. When one mirror faces another, you can see into infinity. If you, as a human, are a mirror and all your Pleiadian selves are a mirror, let yourself feel the fractal of energy into infinity. You can pause as long as you wish before moving on.

- A slight shift in the work happens now, when you are ready. From the infinite mirrors of the Golden Lake comes one fractal you. This is another version of your fractal consciousness. This other you is here to work with you in your present life. Sense this other you. It could be another you from a future time on Earth or a you from the stars. It does not matter. Allow this you to step forward and interact in whatever way is appropriate for this moment. Pause as long as you wish.

- Now become aware of your small physical self. You, as a human being, are one fractal of the whole. Be aware of the you in a body in your room. Be aware of the sensations of energy from this exercise. This energy will continue in your dream state to help you understand yourself as one drop and the whole Lake at the same time. As you go to bed tonight, let yourself think back to the sound of waves on the shore. The Pleiadian transmission will continue, as will your journey deep into your consciousness. When you are ready, in your own time, you may conclude this meditation.

Understanding Comes with Experience

As we discussed previously, the Ama Group came to your world in ancient days and worked primarily in Japan in the areas of Lake Biwa, Lake Towada, and the Okinawan islands, as well as in other areas around the world. Returning to this idea of myth, many gods and goddesses in Japan have the sound "ama" in their names. There is Amaterasu and also Amamikiyo from the Okinawan island chain.

In ancient times, people recognized that our presence on your world was normal and natural. During the time we were here, we were not gods or goddesses; we were simply teachers. After we left and time passed, myths grew. Then we were labeled as gods. The same thing happened around your world with many ET groups.

For us, it is a privilege to be here. The Ama group went back to the light, or the Lake, millennia ago, but from time to time, we communicate with you. We are back again now because of this crucial time on Earth. But our interactions with you are no longer physical, since we are not physical.

As Sasha has said, to transcend polarity and go through this turbulent time, the teachings of the Golden Lake must awaken once again from within you. These teachings are emerging in different forms. They have been given on your Earth since ancient times by different ET groups. The teachings have different flavors, depending on the group, but the core essence is the same.

There is a bit of a paradox with these teachings. The deeper you go into the Golden Lake teachings, the deeper you travel into a realm not ruled by ego. But you are physical beings who still have the anchor of ego, and the mind demands understanding. The mind wants to grab it and look at it under a microscope. When you obsessively examine something, you miss the experience. This is why we have given you some experiential journeys — so you can balance experience with understanding. The most important thing we can say to you is this: When you are confused about a concept and your mind tries to grasp and dissect it, instead seek to experience it. In that experience, true understanding comes.

To some degree, this is a Pleiadian translation of Sirian wisdom. Hamón, the Sirian, tells you to focus on sensation. What he is really saying is to focus on experience. Be fully present with the experience, and through your presence in the experience, understanding will surely come. Understanding is born from within. It does not, and cannot, originate from the mind. If the mind tries to inform experience, the experience itself is not pure. It is a reflection of the mind, which is distorted in physical reality. Experience creates understanding.

The Continuity of Consciousness

Up until now, you have understood the idea that you are one drop of the Lake. But how does consciousness continue? You are also told you have many lives. What links the continuity of lifetimes? Is the drop truly separate from the Lake, having different experiences?

As we talk about the continuity of consciousness, we refer to the flow that happens between lives from the point of view of the Lake. What is that like? How do you become a human? Why do you have the experiences you have as a human? We will explore this as much as we can. We hope to help you tap into an experiential awareness of the fluid and holographic nature of your consciousness.

We will explore these ideas with the help of Sasha, who has a more contemporary understanding of current-day Earth cultures and whose linguistic ability through Lyssa is more refined. Thank you all for sharing this most sacred time with us.

Sasha: Let us return to the teachings of the Lake and the nature of your holographic consciousness. Metaphorically, we have said that the One consciousness is at rest as the Lake. It is calm. There is no conflict, because there is no duality, and it exists in a completely balanced state. But duality is a basic truth of existence once you enter a physical reality, so let us use this symbol [figure 6.1]:

Figure 6.1. The infinity symbol demonstrates where duality crosses.

This is the infinity symbol. The point where the symbol crosses is where duality comes together. That represents the Lake. Existence in a physical reality brings you into a state where energy flows through the cycles of duality. This is natural. You also call it yin and yang.

When the Lake (the One) wishes to experience separation or forgetfulness of its nature, we can metaphorically say that a drop from the Lake moves into physical reality. To extend the metaphor, one of these drops is like your individual soul. Let's say a drop incarnates into a baby, who is born into the world and named Esther. Esther grows and lives her life. Up until now, third-density Esther has viewed herself as singular; she is separated. Esther is not her friend Toshi. Esther is another drop, but she is also the Lake. In third density, she doesn't recognize her connection to the lake. As her consciousness evolves, she begins to sense the truth of its nature — that she and Toshi are the same One consciousness of the Lake, even while having an illusionary experience of separation.

When we use these types of metaphors, we are challenged by linearity. Let us return to the idea of the concentric circles that depict the idea of the relationship between the One and separated reality.

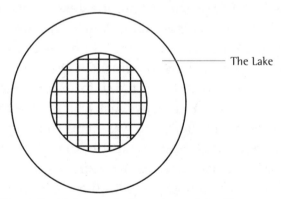

The Lake

Figure 6.2. The relationship between the One and separated reality.

The outer circle, the One consciousness, is the Lake. Thus, when a drop is born as a human, even though it appears to move into a reality of separation, it never really leaves the Lake. There is nowhere to go separate from the Lake. The Lake contains it all, including the realms of separation. So when Esther lives her life and then her life is over, what happens? She is already in the Lake, so where does she go?

Simply, Esther's drop dissolves back into the Lake, which is a metaphorical way of saying that her experience shifts from one of separation to one of holographic awareness.

When Esther was physical, she had an ego that defined her as Esther. But now she is dissolved back into the Lake. So where is the singular person known as Esther? Is there an Esther that still remains separate in the Lake? The answer is no.

In the ancient days, when ETs arrived and began to teach, these were your first spiritual teachings. We had to remember that humanity was young. Intellectually, humans were not as developed as you are now, and you were just beginning your spiritual level of development in these bodies. The teachings were still holographic in nature, but they were much more simplistic. Then something interesting happened.

Your ET teachers delivered the teachings, and then they left. You spent many thousands of years on your own. This is a very crucial time for any species because of what happens to the accuracy of those teachings after the teachers leave. When your Galactic Family left, they usually left behind beings who played roles similar to priests or priestesses. These priests and priestesses encouraged humanity to remember the teachings. But as humanity moved deeper and deeper into separation and the anchor of the ego got heavier and heavier, the accuracy of the teachings diminished. They begin distorting. Egos got more involved, and you started to form religions that became man-made spirituality. You know what happened after that. Wars began over whose belief about God was right. You forgot that the source of all teachings was the same no matter the religion. This was very typical for third-density species. Your species then went through a long period of separation and forgetfulness. Teachers and priests began to distort the teachings unintentionally, and these distortions grew exponentially.

Death and Rebirth

The Golden Lake teachings became distorted, especially about the death and rebirth process. Death and rebirth began to be understood through the lens of the ego. The ego's version of the story was that after death, you go into a kind of energetic limbo. You get reincarnated over and over again. The ego's understanding of reincarnation in the old way was more egoic, because the ego cannot imagine a reality in which it doesn't exist. So the ego believes it is the one reincarnating, thus seeking a kind of continuity in its experience. Distortion grows even more, until your understanding of reincarnation becomes totally egocentric.

Let's say one person, Nancy, believes she was a famous person, like Cleopatra. But Susan also believes she was Cleopatra. Now their egos have a conundrum. "Only one of us can be the real Cleopatra!" This is a linear egoic understanding of the reincarnation process. This is the way humanity came to understand their spiritual connections as you went deep into fragmentation. But again, this is normal and natural for a separated, third-density species. Because humans no longer understood nonlinear spirituality, simpler religions took over the narrative.

You are now in the beginning phases of crossing the threshold into fourth density. Intense separation can no longer be completely maintained. Energy is moving toward integration, and that means you eventually become less ego-driven. It also means you once again become aware of the truth of nonlinear spirituality.

Now let's revisit the Golden Lake teachings from this perspective. Esther finishes her life and doesn't go anywhere, because she is already in the Golden Lake. The soul's energy that formed into the Esther-person now dissolves back into the Golden Lake. It becomes One once again. What happened to Esther's ego?

Remember, we said that the ego functions like an anchor. It exists to keep you grounded in a separated state. Thus, when Esther has no need to be Esther anymore, the ego anchor dissolves. She cannot take it back to the Lake. For many people, this ruins the theory of reincarnation. In the old understanding, continuity is based on a kind of spiritual ego that says, "I was 'this' person, then 'that' person, then 'that' person, and so on." This kind of linear expression is not how things work in the Lake.

Let's present another point of view. At her death, Esther's drop dissolves back into the Lake. There is no more Esther as an identifiable, singular being. But now another part of the Lake wants to experience a physical life, so it forms into a drop and incarnates. Because everything Esther has experienced has been reabsorbed into the Lake, whatever emerges from the Lake will have the imprint of Esther in addition to everyone else's singular experience. This is the holographic nature of the Lake.

Let's call this new drop Thomas. Thomas comes from the Lake and lives his life. He has the imprint of Esther's experiences and the experiences of every other drop that experienced singularity. Is Thomas really unique? What influences him? If Thomas believes he has some past-life issues that need healing, where does that come from? It does not come from the linear continuation of Thomas's other lives, because the ego isn't continuous in that way. The pattern must come from the Lake itself.

This feeling of connection with other lives comes from an energetic pattern in the Lake that is still unresolved; it somehow needs clearing or healing. We can't say it needs resolving because Thomas was killed in a past life, for example, because there is no linear continuity of ego identity in that way. What we can say is that some drop was killed, and some drop still carries the pain or unfinished thing from that life. But Thomas doesn't own it; it is part of the Lake.

When the drop that eventually became Thomas emerged from the Lake, the particular unfinished energy in the Lake — carried in every drop — switched on so this drop named Thomas would play out that specific energy. We go back to the idea we have stated over and over: You are all a complete hologram. You have all the unresolved patterns of singular existence within you on a collective level. Individual drops get triggered to process specific patterns. But no ego owns its pain. It all belongs to the Lake.

We know this might be a confusing concept. Maybe some of your egos are thinking, "Why should I have to clear somebody else's stuff?" Of course, that is a thought from the ego and not based on the reality of One consciousness.

You cannot escape the fact that you are all the Lake. What you experience in this life affects the collective. Everything you experience gets reabsorbed into the Lake, and those who emerge singularly from the Lake with brand-new egos are affected by what the other drops in the Lake have experienced. This is how one drop can make a difference. It is also how evolution progresses.

Again, we often find language challenging because the only way we can describe this is to use language that implies drops are separate from the Lake. What a paradox! Just know this all happens simultaneously. The in-breath and out-breath of the universal Lake represents the drops taking form and then returning to the Lake. There is no story. No ego is involved. That is also how we used the infinity symbol above. Your true state of consciousness — the Lake — is in the center where the loops meet. It is always at rest as the One.

The drops from the Lake emerge in a grand harmony, where all individual beings carry the complete hologram but play out only a part of it. All parts become vital to a dance of wholeness that the singular ego usually can't see. Imbalance is impossible.

The drops emerging from the Lake have imprints that you might consider wounds or karma. The lives in which these drops incarnate play out the dramas necessary to resolve the unresolved patterns for the whole. Drops from the Lake even emerge that do not take on dominant egoic form — people such as Buddha or Jesus, for example. They had physical bodies; thus they still played out the duality of being a drop with an ego and the awakened Lake simultaneously. The Buddha is the story of Siddhartha — a prince who struggled with earthly things until he awakened. When he awakened, he began expressing the consciousness of the Lake through the vehicle of Siddhartha's body. The same was true for Jesus the man and Jesus the Christ. The same is true for all of you. You all have the potential to remember and express the holographic consciousness through your human life. Buddha, Jesus, and others attempted to show you the way.

On countless worlds, this cycle plays out. All drops from the Lake in physical form have the potential for awakened consciousness. Are those awakened drops special? Are they shinier? No, they are not special. Every drop carries the potential for full awakening to Lake consciousness.

The ego might say, "I want to be one of those awakened drops." But the ego cannot control or pursue awakening. This is another paradox. In many of the fourth-density teachings we have shared, we have discussed how the process of awakening is not a doing; it is actually a process of not-doing. The ego fears the state of not-doing because it sees its function coming to a close.

When we talk about not-doing, we do not mean sitting on the couch and drinking beer. We mean a state of allowance and openness that compels you to move with the flow of the universe in a way that is not ego directed. Most of you who have had awakening experiences know they come when you are in a state of allowance and not when you are chasing them. Moving with the flow is a foundational essence of the Golden Lake teachings.

When individual drops emerge from the Lake, they express whatever is needed by the One. Then they return to the Lake. There is no hierarchy, story, or self-importance. Everything is completely balanced at all times, which is so hard for the ego to accept when faced with things it does not like or understand.

To remember this idea, we remind you of the properties of a hologram. If you have a photo of an apple on holographic film and you tear that photo into tiny pieces, you can never destroy the photo of the apple. The image of the apple just gets smaller and smaller on the film. The apple is always complete. This is the consciousness of the Golden Lake. Even the smallest drop carries the complete experience of the Lake.

This is your true nature. Your existence as third-density beings for so many thousands of years has blinded you with the eyes of separation. Again, this is a normal part of evolution. Now that you are moving into fourth density and beginning your awakening process, you are sensing the infinite nature of your being outside the realm of duality. Keep going. As we have said, it is not an intellectual process but an experiential one. Open yourself to the Lake, for it is All That Is. It is the One. It is you.

SEVEN

The Spaces Between: Introducing the Quantum Map

SASHA

W e have been talking about holographic consciousness using the metaphor of the Golden Lake. Knowing this informa- tion intellectually can help prepare you for the experience, but simple knowledge cannot take the place of experience. Through the contact work we have done with many of you over several decades, we have helped provide you with an experiential framework through which you can connect with your holographic nature. As you stretch your consciousness beyond limited physical reality, you also connect with other beings whose natural states of consciousness are more holographic. Very often, these other beings you meet during contact work are like other aspects of you — what you might call your future selves, if you look at it in a limited, linear way.

We will explore holographic reality and its relationship to physi- cal reality to help you understand how human consciousness evolves in a very distinct way. For the purposes of this discussion, we will use the labels "human reality" and "ET reality" to contrast their differences. Human reality tends to be more separate, represented by the distinct divisions in your brain wave states that show the different ways you perceive reality.

ET reality is a more integrated state of consciousness, more inclusive of all aspects of reality in a multidimensional way. Humans experience a strong sense of separation between "me" and "the universe," so you don't yet fully see yourselves as multidimensional. But when you do contact work or even deep meditation, your perspective begins to unlock from separation. You move into a perception of your consciousness as a unified field containing what seem to be other consciousnesses as well. This is one of the main reasons we do this work with you.

Contact Training 2014

In some of our contact trainings, our intention is to help you enter what we call the quantum fabric. This refers to a metaphorical energetic fabric that is nonlinear, nonpolarized, and nonhierarchical. You could say it is the beginning step in moving into holographic consciousness. It is inclusive of all consciousness that is capable of resonating at these integrative levels. When we do these trainings, you often notice that environmental conditions mirror the lesson we arrange for that night. Following is an example of what we mean:

At a training in Japan in 2014, the group arrived at the contact site. The site was a large field in a remote area near Mt. Fuji. A light rain did not keep students from seeing the whole field when they arrived. The group set up their gear and settled in to begin contact work. As contact work began, the quantum fog arrived. On the surface it looked like regular fog, but it was more than that. It was perfectly timed to the work we were doing with the group, and it was part of the lesson. The fog became so thick that group members could not see each other. As a result, they could not use their eyes to navigate reality. They had no choice but to go within and expand their consciousness of the inner landscape. Participants experienced the entire contact lesson for that night in that quantum fog, and it was a profound lesson for many. Human, interstellar, and interdimensional consciousnesses met together. As soon as the contact work ended, the fog disappeared. This happened predictably during several sequential contact retreats.

For decades, we have talked about what we call internal navigation. It is a way to navigate reality based on internal experience rather than external perception. We have said that this skill is necessary for true space travel. During these lessons in the quantum fog, groups were given the opportunity to shut off 3D perception and expand consciousness into quantum perception. This is necessary for the evolution of consciousness on this world and for Earth's eventual initiation into the cosmic multidimensional community.

A common Hollywood perspective of contact is humans and ETs meeting and shaking hands, and then the ETs magically conform to human reality. Those types of meetings cannot occur until human consciousness shifts to be more compatible with the default universal consciousness that is holographic in nature. The movie *Arrival* approached this idea. We have given you trainings to help you take those small steps.

The Structure of Reality and the Quantum Map

The following discussion on the structure of reality is a simplistic way to guide you to holographic realms and to help you understand this journey that is about to unfold in human consciousness. As you experientially remember your true state of consciousness, you will reconnect with the bigger community of consciousness that includes more expanded versions of yourself. This evolutionary process can be plotted along a metaphorical map that represents the journey from illusionary separation back to the One. Through this discourse, we will begin building this Quantum Map and explain as we go along.

- -

Figure 7.1. The dashed line represents the human experience of separation.

Here we have drawn a dashed line [figure 7.1]. Think of those old-fashioned movie projectors, when movies were on rolls of film. When you stretch out the film, you see many picture frames. When the film is played at a certain speed on the projector, the story appears seamless. You no longer see a series of still photos with spaces between them; you see a fluid story.

Physical reality is similar. Your true state of awareness is actually whole and observes physical reality as shown in figure 7.2.

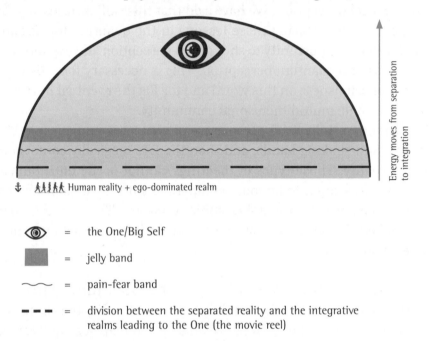

🌀 ⚓ 👤👤👤👤👤 Human reality + ego-dominated realm

Energy moves from separation to integration

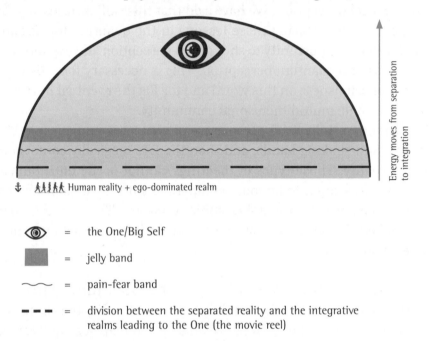 = the One/Big Self

▪ = jelly band

〜 = pain-fear band

▪ ▪ ▪ = division between the separated reality and the integrative realms leading to the One (the movie reel)

Figure 7.2. Given by Sasha, this is the Quantum Map, which demonstrates the true state of awareness. To learn more about the Quantum Map, please see our series of YouTube videos. The first one can be found at: https://youtu.be/WexsOj98mwk. More in-depth recordings are also available with these teachings at LyssaRoyal.net.

Think of reality as one big cycle of breath. On the in-breath, consciousness is whole and holographic (the eye in the diagram). On the out-breath, consciousness projects into physical reality and experiences an illusion of separation. Experiences of separation have gaps between them, like the gaps between the frames of a movie reel. When consciousness experiences the limited reality of third or early fourth density, it is anchored by the ego, whose job is to maintain separation. Separated consciousness can't perceive the true nature of its existence. But as you work to expand consciousness, such as through meditation or contact work, you begin to perceive the spaces between the movie frames of physical reality. In those spaces, you will find your true holographic consciousness. Understanding this concept is the first step to conscious navigation on the Quantum Map.

A spectrum of exponentially integrated consciousness exists between the separated state and the fully awakened state. Meditation and contact work trains you to sense this spectrum of consciousness, and this is why it is so important at this time in human evolution.

Different Expressions of the Same Form

Your quantum physicists have seen that physical reality seems to exist and then not exist. They don't yet know why, but they are getting closer to understanding that the universe and consciousness are actually expressions of the same thing in different forms.

We can only explain this in metaphor, but let us address how change happens in physical reality. Energy cycles constantly from formlessness to form in a process similar to breathing in and out. The in-breath represents the spaces between bursts of materiality. On that imperceptible in-breath, consciousness moves back to the One, during which the energetic template of the necessary experience gets recalibrated to be exactly a reflection of the person experiencing separated consciousness. So on the next metaphorical out-breath, consciousness moves back to form, and reality aligns with the energy of the experience in a way that reflects your consciousness.

It isn't a matter of a higher being telling you what you need to experience. It is simple energy dynamics. You have heard the phrase that if you want to change reality, you have to change yourself. This is what that means. Thus, two perceptions happen simultaneously:

- the perception of physical reality by the human being, which is incomplete and based on illusion even though it seems fluid
- the perception of the One, the eye in the diagram, the real you who sees the whole movie reel simultaneously

When you do contact work with us, you move into the cosmic in-breath, so to speak. You travel between the spaces of the movie reel into the eternal now. When you move into that state, you can feel the allness of the One. This means that other beings that also exist in that state can more easily connect with you. It is truly a common ground.

It is becoming essential for humanity to learn to sense and consciously experience the spaces between the movie frames. When you do, it unlocks you from the anchor of the ego. This allows your consciousness to dramatically shift, and you begin to cultivate a more universal perspective. Of course, we do not recommend that you abandon your human perspective. We recommend that you learn to integrate the two. This is the phase of evolution in which the small self and the Big Self (the One, the the Big Eye on the map) begin to integrate. It is like learning to surf the in-breath and the out-breath. As you do, you teach yourself to maintain the Big Self perspective for longer and longer, which facilitates more integration of the Big and small selves.

This new consciousness won't happen in its entirety tomorrow, but those of you already practicing are the pioneers who will make it easier for those who come after you. As you learn to operate in these two states of consciousness simultaneously, the visions you have about a galactic community will more easily come to pass.

This material we share helps you acclimate to these more integrated quantum states. But what happens if we closely examine this progression into quantum consciousness? You find a gradation of energy, where consciousness becomes more and more integrated, with important nexus points along the way. You might recognize some of those nexus points on the Quantum Map.

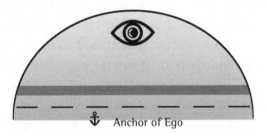

Figure 7.3. The basic foundation of the Quantum Map.

In figure 7.3, the dashed line with the ego anchor below represent human reality. The thick gray line is the first nexus point you encounter as you learn to ride the in-breath and out-breath of quantum reality. This line represents an energy that can be likened to petroleum jelly. The best way to describe it is through experience.

When you do deep meditation or contact work, many of you experience a heavy, sluggish energy that can make you sleepy or spacey. It feels almost as if you are moving through jelly. This is quite normal and represents an entrance point into quantum energy. It serves a function similar to that of an airlock. If you were able to move your consciousness farther up on the diagram, water would be added to the jelly, and it would become more easily navigable.

Continuing with the metaphor, the energy feels watery. Going up even farther, it feels like steam and then finally like pure energy or liquid light as you approach the One. You don't have to worry about how to navigate these layers. It is a natural process that happens when the time is right, and it cannot be navigated by the ego. We simply use these examples to help you understand how consciousness refines as it moves toward the One. There is a spectrum of consciousness that moves from a denser state (the human level) to a more rarified state (the One).

As you go deeper into this state of quantum consciousness, the human mind often experiences paradox. This is a good sign that you are unlocking from linear and polarized reality. One of the first tests as you navigate this terrain is how you respond to paradox. The mind exists in the realm of polarity, and when it experiences two opposites that are both true, it tries to invalidate the experience or choose a side. For example, you might think, "How can I be a single person and the One simultaneously?" This is the first obstacle. If the mind stays stuck in paradox, consciousness cannot go further. The heart is the gateway through which paradox is resolved. We will talk more about paradox soon.

As you move further into quantum reality, polarity-orientation begins to disappear. You experience the dual nature of reality as the separated small self and the One Big Self simultaneously. As you move through paradox, the anchor of the ego gets lighter. This state of consciousness is necessary for contact with other loving beings of similar consciousness and direct aspects of you that you call parallel or future lives. Ultimately, as you traverse this quantum map, you recognize that no one is actually separated and outside the Big Self. You fully understand the experience of Oneness beyond the mind. As we said, the quantum map has nexus points, and we will discuss their importance when the time is right. For now, you can say that encountering paradox serves a great purpose, because your mind eventually gets so tired that it has the opportunity to surrender so that your consciousness can go even deeper.

Quantum Physics Seen through Linear Knowledge

I believe ET science is really different from human science. Do you have theories and then use a process to prove the theory?

Not that way, no. The human way is to find a theory, which usually becomes a headache. Maybe inspiration comes from that eventually. For humans, you start with the head; when you have inspiration from your heart or deeper awareness, you bring it back to the head. You end up invalidating what you intuitively felt was true. For us, we always see consciousness as the most basic part of the equation. Mathematics or science is an expression of consciousness. That isn't very understandable by the human mind right now, but it is coming. From quantum knowledge — the higher realms on the quantum map — we know how to, in a sense, stretch truth into linearity, drop it through the spaces between the quantum and 3D, and apply it in physical reality.

Right now on your world, most cutting-edge science is based on quantum theory. Scientists can sense an immense breakthrough, but they keep bringing it back to the mind. They see strange things in quantum realms. For example, how can particles exist in two places at the same time? But because they cannot embrace a seeming paradox, they cannot apply quantum knowledge to a linear reality. Quantum realms still intrigue them, so they keep going back to learn more, making them more confused. Eventually, they will see that linear thinking is like building a road with a dead end. Most likely, in a moment of insight and when the time is right, they will see the whole structure of reality clearly. That time is coming.

When quantum physics started on Earth, perhaps 100 years ago, was it inspired by Pleiadian knowledge?

In our observation, quantum physics didn't begin on Earth 100 years ago. In the ancient days of your world, philosophy, science, mathematics, geometry, and spirituality were all considered one thing. Quantum understanding was present because the understanding of consciousness was present. As your world entered an evolutionary cycle of separation, those branches of quantum understanding also began to separate. Math, science, religion, and philosophy became separate ideas. You cannot understand the whole from a separated part.

Now that you have entered an evolutionary cycle of integration, it is as if these separate compartments are beginning to flow together. This creates breakthroughs in quantum theory. Scientists are sensing the interconnectedness of these previously separate parts, but they haven't yet put the full puzzle together. The underlying energy that connects all the parts is consciousness. They are just starting to understand that, but they don't know how to investigate it. This is the missing piece, so to speak, but so far it seems to be the least likely place to investigate. That will eventually change, and your scientists will start seeing the connectivity between all things. This is a natural step for all developing civilizations: Consciousness and science become one.

You spoke about quantum consciousness and human polarized consciousness below the dashed line. You said it is like an in-breath and an out-breath and that change happens continually in conjunction with this cycle. How many times per second does this doorway for change occur? Are we being reborn into another version of ourselves?

It cannot be measured because the mind cannot perceive it. The interval is so small that the brain cannot process it. But from the quantum perspective, consciousness can perceive how stretched out linear reality is, and the spaces are easily perceived. At this point in evolution, the human mind is not able to perceive this. You can say that with each breath, you are indeed being reborn into another version of you.

How does energetic acceleration affect the human body? Does it accelerate or slow the aging process?

The biggest difference is that on the meta-atomic level, your cells become able to hold more chi — also known as ki or prana. Let us use an analogy. Thirty to forty years ago, solar energy technology was not as advanced as it is today. Solar cells could only absorb and process a limited amount of sunlight and thus distribute only a small charge. That has now changed, but solar energy technology still has a long way to go. The body is the same.

In third density, your body's primary source of fuel is food. As you move further into fourth density and your energy accelerates, you become more like we Pleiadians. You become less reliant on physical food and more reliant on chi or prana — the energy of the universe fuels your cells. This isn't anything you can force. You cannot try to survive on chi alone as a spiritual practice until your body and consciousness are ready.

It is important to pay attention to your body and give it what it needs. We have spoken to many people lately who are having dramatic diet changes that seem to be happening naturally. This is all part of evolution. As to how it affects aging, you will find that your life spans will become longer and your bodies will become more and more stable, especially when you work out your emotional issues and stop storing pain in your bodies.

Traveling the Quantum Map

In the diagram of the quantum map, we talked about the jelly band. Looking at it as a frequency spectrum, this jelly band is the area in which many physical ETs who contact you hang out. This band of energy is where consciousness can easily go back and forth between physical and quantum expressions.

We also talked about how the ego is like an anchor. When the anchor is really heavy, as it is in third density, you experience reality in a linear way. When you experience linear time, you are not as aware that anything more is "out there" unless you have a dream or some type of spiritual experience. As a species begins to move out of third density and into fourth — as you are doing now — you increase your ability to travel to this jelly band through expansions of your consciousness during contact work or meditation. As you learn to move into quantum states of consciousness, you make it easier for other members of your species to do so later on. You pave the road, so to speak.

With this said, you can imagine that advanced ET beings who exist closer to the jelly band might find it very difficult to drop into a linear reality to meet with you. It actually takes them a lot of energy and focus to do this, and it is not very comfortable. This is one reason UFO sightings are so frustrating for many of you, because they don't seem to conform to the laws of physical reality. The human level of reality is not the normal state of existence for occupants of ET crafts, so chasing UFOs and demanding evidence that conforms to physical definitions of reality is a bit of a dead end. The more efficient method of contact is to meet on a common ground of consciousness — a realm that is actually a natural state for both of you, even if you are only now beginning to remember that state.

Let's say that your species begins to establish relationships with ETs, and connecting in these quantum states becomes easier. We mentioned how there is a gradation of energy on the quantum map, where the thick jelly becomes more like liquid and moves through different states all the way to pure energy. Each state of the quantum reflects the level of consciousness that inhabits it.

As a human exploring contact, you have the ability, with practice, to shift your consciousness to align with the jelly band. This is where you can meet groups of ETs with physical bodies who are members of your galactic family. With practice, you will have the ability to move into more refined energy bands of the quantum. What will you find there? Consciousness is less individualized, and you will meet beings who are more plasmic in nature.

The Arcturians are good examples of plasmic beings. Even though they might show themselves to you in a body form, that is not how they self-identify. They are moving toward group expression, but they will often show themselves to you as a singular being to make it easier for you. Even saying the word "group" is not correct, because if I say, "These four people are a group," you still think of them as four individuals. When we talk about the group consciousness of Arcturus, there are really no words to describe what we mean. It is beyond the idea of a bunch of individuals in a group.

If you keep going upward on the quantum map, you will continue to see different gradations that create more comprehensive collective-consciousness systems. We very often use archetypes to express this idea, as we did with the Arcturians. We also use the archetype of the Founders to express the idea of a very integrated collective consciousness that represents the first fragmentation from the source, to look at it in a linear way. These Founders often appear as tall, willowy, skinny beings. Sometimes they appear as insects. Despite this archetypal imagery, these beings have such a limited relationship to physical reality that body image is just a way to express themselves in a way humans can understand.

When you move even more deeply into quantum consciousness, what do you experience? We will have to use a metaphor again. Water is a very useful one. Consciousness at this level is like water. The imagery of a body becomes a limiting concept. Water is limitless and fluid and can expand into infinity.

You Are Both Separate and One

On the quantum level, your consciousness is like water, which we've defined as the Golden Lake. As water, the only way to see yourself, or separated aspects of yourself, is to look inside. Take the example of an aquarium. It is filled with water and has fish inside. The water is your quantum nature, and in order to experience and learn from separation, you create aspects of you inside yourself. The fish, sand, and fake plastic seaweed are all within your quantum consciousness. They seem separate, but in reality, they cannot ever be separated from the water because they are within it. All the separate aspects inside the water are different expressions of the quantum, expressed according to the frequency at which they express themselves.

The idea that anything can really be separate from you is impossible. This is the core paradox — that you are both separate and the One. Thus, when you encounter other forms of life on the quantum map, they are still like the fish in the aquarium. They are still part of the One, watery quantum consciousness that is all that exists. This is one of the core lessons of contact work. With repeated experiences of traveling through the quantum map, it becomes crystal clear that there is no entity in the universe that isn't another expression of you — not the ego-identified you, but the One quantum you.

In that One quantum state, there is no duality. This is why fragmentation happened. From that high state of quantum Oneness, there is only emptiness. If the One wants a new experience and wants to see itself in myriad ways, it must create fragmentation within itself in order to see itself. You cannot see your own face without a mirror. When Onenss created the illusion that something was separate from it, it could have a whole growth experience that was impossible from the state of Oneness.

Religions tell you humankind fell. No, no, no. You cannot fall from one place to another, because you exist on all levels at all times. Using metaphor again, we can say that as fragmentation happened, the Big

Self began to see through infinite eyes. You have eyes on every level, including your physical human eyes that convince you that you are separate. Your ego — the organizer of the most separated reality — convinces you that physicality is the dominant reality. But the version of you with eyes on other levels knows the reality construct is much more vast and that human reality is a small percentage of experience.

We spoke about the ego as an anchor. In its essence, it is neutral and performs an important function. As you learn to shift your attention away from the ego anchor as being the primary experience of reality, the anchor begins to lighten, and you start to experience yourself on other levels of the quantum. Contact work and meditation are hugely integrative processes, for they get you in touch with other aspects of your consciousness.

Even though you might contact what appear to be separate ET beings in the jelly band, this model provides a fun way to interact with them as if they are separate from you. A quantum contact experience is truly an integration of another aspect of you. It is like drops of the lake experiencing a reunion. If you remember five contact experiences you've had over your lifetime, you are actually always connected to these other aspects of you in every moment, even if you are unaware of it. You make these types of connections continuously; this is natural. But as a human with a singular ego in physical reality, you would feel way too disoriented if you lived in several realities at once. Thus, the singular identification is useful for this reality.

As you begin to develop the ability to move more and more into quantum consciousness, the anchor gets lighter, and your perception of reality changes. Your perception become more fluid. It becomes similar to those experienced by other beings existing near the quantum jelly band. This is when you begin to unlock from a limited reality and your consciousness expands.

You might ask, "How can I train myself to have these kinds of experiences?" You might be tempted to use substances to do this, but that is not something we recommend, because substances strengthen the belief that you need something outside yourself to move into quantum consciousness. That is not true. The best way is to do what you can to lighten the anchor and experiment with ways to experience your quantum consciousness, such as through meditation or contact work. At times, your mind might try to invalidate your experiences, or you might experience doubt. This is natural. Don't let it stop you from exploring. At some point, your cumulative experiences will be enough to wear down the doubt.

Your Protectors from Sirius

As you continue to move more into fourth density, the beings who work with Earth as your guides will begin to change. We wish to talk about the Sirian named Hamón. As you know, Sirians played a very important role in human development. The Sirian commitment to humans borders on obsessive, and we mean this in a lighthearted way. They made a commitment in ancient days to help uplift human-kind. That commitment spans eons, both genetically and spiritually. They've always watched over you, but their energy is very active at this transitional time. It is no coincidence that you call Sirius the Dog Star, for Sirians are loyal in that way.

In my reality, Hamón is an ambassador and a kind of celebrity. He is well known and widely respected, because he carries the lineage of the ancient loyalty to Earth — the first Sirians who came to Earth as your protectors and teachers. They have been training your consciousness for a long time. At this time on Earth, he is very excited about your growing ability to move into quantum-energy bands. This is one of the signs the Sirians look for. When they see this ability begin to blossom, they know the species is getting ready to make a huge leap. It is truly a cause for celebration in our galactic family.

We know some of you have made jokes about his name. No, it is not Spanish for "ham" or "pork." In the ancient priestly language of the Sirians, it is the closest word or sound a human can make to express the meaning of integration. He was given the name during his training and awakening process eons ago. It expresses his commitment to guiding humanity through their integration process.

We Pleiadians and Sirians are like your older cousins. We are much more connected to you than you realize. Sirian energy is rising in the consciousness of humans, and many of you are experiencing contacts and memories of the ancient past. As we continue with these transmissions, more and more teachings will come from Hamón and the Sirian perspective.

When the body is sleeping are our consciousnesses in the quantum?

When you sleep, there is no anchor; you go back into your natural state. You experience the complete disconnection of the anchor, but a ghost anchor remains that keeps you tethered, so to speak. Let us give you an example of what we mean: During a dream, you are fully immersed in the dream experience. Then a thought comes into your dream, such as, "What time is it?" or "I shouldn't do that." These are thoughts the ego anchor usually has. This is what we mean by the ghost anchor. You might have an overlay of your physical persona in the dream state. If you are interested in learning about the habits and patterns of the ego, look to your dreams, because you can see them revealed. The patterns clearly play out in your dreams.

So, yes, your consciousness is, in essence, in the quantum state when you sleep. It is really interesting that humans require so much sleep. It takes a lot of energy to focus in physical reality. Because of this, you require a lot of recharging. ETs whose states of consciousness are closer to the jelly band, including my species, don't sleep the same way you do, because our consciousness is more integrated. We more easily tap into quantum energy to recharge.

As you transition from third to fourth density and train yourself to move into quantum realms, your relationship to sleep will begin to change. Some of you might need less; some might need more. Sleep could be erratic for a while. If you have trouble sleeping but you are exhausted, you might be resisting moving into the quantum. Your ego doesn't like losing control until it learns to relax with a new experience.

EIGHT

Emotions and the Quantum Map

SASHA

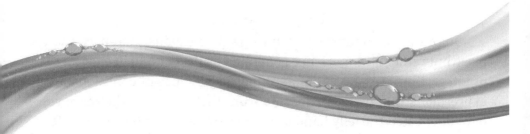

Let us explore the quantum map more deeply. This metaphor is a way to help you understand what happens with the awakening process in the context of your physical life. As you become more comfortable experiencing these quantum states of consciousness, deeper levels of reintegration occur with your quantum self, which includes other aspects of you that you might call your galactic selves — what you see as other, separate lifetimes in the cosmos.

On the quantum map, we referred to the entry points into the quantum, which are shown as gaps in a dashed line. We also talked about the in-breath (when consciousness moves back to the source) and the out-breath (when consciousness projects into physical reality). As a human, you don't see this constant disassembling and reassembling of reality.

When you are in a conscious process of spiritual work and growth and you release old patterns that keep you stuck and learn to see reality with the Big Eye (from the perspective of the One), this process disassembles the old ego construct and reassembles a new one more aligned with these new changes. (This is not a conscious process run by the ego.) The new ego construct has less baggage and moves you toward what you call awakening.

Another significant byproduct of this work is that as you become more comfortable operating in an integrated state, you perceive and experience reality from the perspective of a single, nondual eye rather than a polarized, double eye. The ego then goes through a transformation: It becomes a more nondual organizer of reality rather than a polarized interpreter of reality. As that happens, you are more able to connect with other beings on the quantum map who also resonate at this more integrated frequency.

The Ego Anchor

Quantum consciousness is universal consciousness. It is not a place but rather an experience generated by deeper and deeper levels of integration. It is a common ground for all types of consciousness expressions that can also operate from that state. On the map, we have delineated the jelly band as the place where you first encounter this more integrated state of consciousness [see figure 8.1].

You have all chosen to have a life as a human. Part of the contract, so to speak, is that you have an anchor (the ego) that keeps you present in this illusion of separation. The ego is a neutral mechanism with no negative intent. But sometimes the methods by which the ego keeps you anchored can be painful. The first challenge on the quantum map has to do with helping the ego let go of the linear time stream and feel more comfortable releasing its fixed sense of reality in which things must be controlled in order for it to relax.

The ego doesn't see the entry points into quantum consciousness, but it senses a vague threat and tries to protect you from leaving the secure reality it has created for you. This is often the biggest challenge to awakening. Many get stuck here, lost in illusion. This is why we shared the School of the Nine Serpents, as a system that helped your Galactic Family move beyond illusion into their awakening process.

Once you train yourself to move through those illusionary ego structures, you enter a whole new reality on the quantum map. To use a metaphor, it is like being on a beach where the shore slopes down into the water. First you put your toes in the water, then your ankles, and then your knees. You go deeper and deeper until the environment completely changes: It no longer resembles the original environment. The same is true for the quantum map. As you do this work, you might feel a sense of disorientation as well as a sense of familiarity, because your consciousness moves from solid form into liquid energy. This can be very disorienting and also very freeing.

Once you unlock from the ego state on the quantum map, consciousness moves into a quasi-liquid state that is like jelly: the jelly band. In this metaphor, you can say that this jelly-like state causes you to slow down, and it gives you a chance to integrate the energy. You no longer experience linear reality. You have to be fully present at each stage. There is no past or future in this state outside linear time, and you have to bring your energy to a single point of focus within your consciousness. Here, you relax and become more present.

If you keep going on the quantum map into higher states of integration, the energy gets even more refined. It becomes thinner and more like liquid. Then it transitions from fluid to pure energy in the higher states on the quantum map.

As you enter and then pass through the jelly band, you perceive that consciousness slows down. No mental or physical awareness keeps you in a constant state of disintegration. Paradox starts to reveal itself. Even though you feel time has slowed, your ability to merge with the universal hologram accelerates. Polarity and duality vanish, and you find that you can experience paradox in a whole new way. (We will talk about this a bit more later).

To continue with the metaphor, as you move more deeply into this state of liquid energy, consciousness starts to display liquid tendencies. Water is known as a universal solvent, and it starts to dissolve the residue from the human experience. To be a bit humorous, we could say that humans have a "crust" around them. This crust is made up of old pains, beliefs, and traumas. All those old painful experiences created the crust as a protective mechanism. As you start to move into the liquid state beyond the jelly, the water begins to dissolve away the crust. As a human having this experience, you feel emotion. If you have been wearing a proverbial suit of armor and it dissolves in front of your eyes, you feel afraid. You feel naked, because all your protection is stripped as you move into the quantum state. You feel extreme vulnerability.

Yes! I discovered that when my heart opens deeply and I feel euphoric, pain becomes much more intense.

Exactly. This is a perfect example of what happens in this process. Your mind has to let go. The linear 3D aspect has to be released to allow more emotion to rise. This process dissolves the crust and brings you more in touch with your emotional body. But when this happens, you might think you are going crazy or that something is wrong with you. You berate yourself and say, "Why am I so sensitive? Something must be wrong with me. My spiritual practice is failing me because I feel this pain." But in reality, a sign of your integration and opening is when you become more sensitive during this adjustment period. If you resist, it lasts a whole lot longer. The evolutionary cycle asks you to slowly drop the armor. Some of you will do it willingly, and others will not.

Look at all the things happening on your world, such as shootings and worldwide stress levels becoming more intolerable. Many of you don't understand what is happening energetically, and you resist it. You don't allow yourself to painfully open, which is necessary for the healing process to take place. No one teaches this to you on your world, so many of you end up having to go through hell until you awaken yourself and understand that this process is much larger than one individual. This is a sign of a species evolution, but it isn't fun. It is the process of moving from polarized consciousness into that Big Eye state of non-duality. It is a big change from the egoic way of navigating through reality, and it requires a lot of disassembling. Many of you have the erroneous belief that the process of awakening or ascension is all about angels singing and unicorns jumping over rainbows.

This is a process of letting go of the old things you thought have protected you. You must move into the universe naked. For those of you who have ever been to a nudist beach, at first you might feel that you don't want to show other people your "stuff." But then you get to the beach and you see that everyone walks around with their stuff on display, and they seem free. The same thing is happening on Earth. When you realize it is okay to show your stuff to yourself and to others, the transformation process begins to take root. Self-love and self-acceptance grow, which is an essential next step.

The Pain-Fear Band

Moving further along the quantum map, we want to look at a layer we call the pain-fear band. Actually, several layers on the quantum map require you to confront your fears and move through your pain. On the map below, we have added a wavy line that represents the pain-fear band.

As you move beyond the ego and head toward the jelly band, you might encounter a paradox: incredible love and joy as well as incredible pain and fear. The emotional pain is just a layer to move through; it is not caused by this experience. The pain is representative of what has protected you from merging back into your true, integrated state of consciousness. When you encounter the pain, it is easy to think you have done something wrong or that a "negative entity" is causing it, but that is not true. It is simply unhealed, unresolved energy — you could call it shadow energy — that you must integrate in your consciousness before you can go deeper into the quantum states of consciousness.

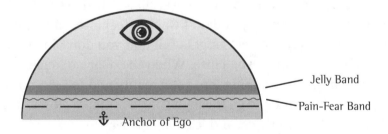

Figure 8.1. The pain-fear band (in the Quantum Map) must be confronted on your way to integrated consciousness.

If you allow yourself to move through the pain or fear and not resist it, you pop through the pain-fear band. Consider this band like a jungle path. The first time through is the hardest, like cutting through a jungle with a machete. Each time you encounter it, the path gets wider and easier to cross. Fear and pain become your teachers, which is a necessary step on the path of integration. If you experience any resistance to this process, your inner guidance keeps you working here until you move on to deeper quantum levels.

The Role of Emotion

What is the role of emotion in quantum consciousness? We have spoken to many people around your world who believe their emotions have become uncontrollable. Do you think you can control your emotions? So many members of your galactic family learned the hard way that it is impossible, and trying to do so prolongs your evolutionary journey. Nevertheless, many of you feel lost and confused because you don't know how to work with the emotional body. You find that when you try to repress emotion, it comes out physically as weird illnesses or body manifestations that are medically hard to treat.

I will now put on my galactic anthropologist hat. If we look at this from a larger perspective as a species manifestation, this is a natural experience for a species in transition. We know it doesn't feel good. We know you don't want to experience pain or feel out of control. Many of you would prefer to have no emotions at all, but part of you knows that repressing emotions isn't the answer.

In the deepest experience of separation in third density, you got used to putting everything you didn't want to feel into a metaphorical closet. At some point, the closet gets full and you don't know what's in there. The door won't even close. When the door no longer closes, the stuff from the closet spills into your reality and forces you to see it. You have to be willing to go through your emotional closet, unpack what has been hidden there, and learn a new way to feel.

When we say this, some of you envision a linear process, such as, "Well, this was 1985. Now I have to do 1986." That is not what we mean. Quantum work is not linear. It is based on a holographic principle. More than anything else, this has to do with giving yourself permission to unpack your emotions and being present for the unpacking.

Emotion often manifests as pure energy. Sometimes you feel emotion energetically, and you don't know what it means or why you feel it. It might have to do with an old trauma, such as a parent's death. Or it could be a current issue, such as a difficult child. If you don't know the origin, that is okay; it is just trapped energy. Other times, you might clearly know why you feel a certain way. The emotional body is layered like an onion.

What is most important is being present with the process of unpacking the energy behind the emotion. That can be as simple as sitting quietly, breathing, being very present, and allowing the energy or emotion to come to the surface. Without resistance, it often washes through you like a wave and just releases.

Part of your evolution as a species also means learning this basic ebb and flow of the emotional body. Emotions are much like the tides on your world. They ebb and flow — and not always with a story attached. In fact, sometimes it is best to let go of the story and just be present with the ebb and flow.

Let's say you want to explore the contact process and travel along the quantum map to higher states of consciousness in order to meet other beings (who are aspects of you). If you have not done the emotional work, it can make the contact process harder, because all the stuff packed in your closet is like a heavy rock. The rock represents a layer that stops you from experiencing your Big Self (the eye on the map). Trying to move to more refined states of consciousness while not having done the emotional healing work is like trying to swim in a suit of armor. It isn't impossible, but it requires a tremendous amount of focus and strength that most of you don't have. Instead of going deep inside, you project your pain onto others, such as saying your ET encounters are negative or your pain is the fault of others. In the end, the pain is much more intense if you choose to ignore it.

If you allow the crust to dissolve through emotional work, what is underneath becomes the new flesh. At the beginning, you are super sensitive, because new flesh is tender and vulnerable. You feel naked, but you eventually get used to it. This is happening right now on the mass consciousness level as well as on the individual level; however, it is sometimes hard to separate the two. You and mass consciousness are very tied together, and this is a very challenging and purging time for you both. When you do this work personally, you energetically pave the way for others within mass consciousness.

We've seen species try to awaken without doing the painful emotional work, and it is very difficult. As humans do this painful work, you begin to cement your reputations as masters of emotion in your future timeline. Move forward with this hard work. Break the shell open, and you will be reborn.

Does this mean that as we begin working in the jelly band, it will be easier for others to experience the jelly band too?

Yes.

So our world in this reality is becoming more emotional?

We want to define what "becoming more emotional" really means. Very often, the ego thinks this means that emotions are uncontrolled and create chaos. We refer to it more in terms of a healthy flow of emotion, an ebb and flow, where you no longer feel shame, resistance, or fear. Instead, you recognize you cannot project this healthy flow of emotion onto others. You own your experience.

When you talked about the Zetas suppressing their emotions, you said they created a lot of pain for themselves. But if they didn't feel emotion, how could they feel the pain they created? I understood that you meant it was their choice to continue to suppress, and once the unrecognized pain got to such an extreme, the energy was intolerable, and they were forced to feel. Is that correct?

Yes, exactly. We have spoken about the Zeta civilization in three eras. The first was the era of their near destruction. They experienced so much pain as they suppressed their emotions that it created their species crisis. The second era was the time of their healing process. They had denied their emotions so much that it finally caused the repressed energy to come to the surface in a way they had to acknowledge. In the third era, they became the evolved Zetas through their healing crisis and subsequent awakening.

These third-era Zetas communicate with many of you at this time, especially in the context of contact work as it relates to the awakening process. Humanity and individuals connect to the Zetas in whatever period of their evolution reflects what you need to see for your evolution. Contact is a mirror in which you see yourself. This is one reason why it is so valuable. ET consciousness always reflects the fearful aspects you haven't owned or integrated.

The idea of repressed emotion isn't really discussed much. I always wonder how this can be resolved as a society. I am always baffled when people talk about detecting mental illness on the news. I think, "How can you not see what the problem is?" No one seems to see the pain underneath human consciousness and work with it on that level.

It is very difficult to diagnose one's own dysfunction, as evidenced by the challenges of your galactic family. Right now, you haven't learned how to see holistically. Your civilization is caught in the pattern of projecting blame onto others, and it is hard to see beyond that. Change has to come at the grassroots level, with each person doing his or her work. This creates momentum, like a snowball rolling down a hill. We realize it is excruciatingly painful to see what is happening on your world and know that, as an individual, all you can do is turn inward and do your work. It can feel like watching grass grow.

To us, we don't mind watching grass grow, and the Sirians especially are masters of it. Evolution is transgenerational: You see a small shift in each generation. This can feel hopeless from the human ego perspective, but when you learn to see with the Big Eye, you start to feel the flow of evolution, and it becomes less frustrating. You realize nothing is wrong, because you move beyond polarized vision. You learn to relax and allow, do only what you are guided to do, and then let go. Nothing is within your control, anyway.

Does astrology, with its eclipses and alignments, represent some type of gateway?

Yes and no. As we have said, nothing generates from outside you. Everything generates from within the One consciousness. This becomes apparent as you begin to feel comfortable in the more refined layers of consciousness on the quantum map. You start to see that what you call synchronicity is an expression of the truth that all things are connected. Everything is locked in a continuous dance of synchronicity. There is no cause and effect in that level of consciousness. Only the mind looks for cause and effect. There is a bigger dance going on. Astrology and other systems show you just a small piece of the interconnectedness of the universe. Like the previous question about mental health, you are still in the process of viewing reality in an interconnected way.

The Emotions of the Awakened Self

We used to think emotions were our own private little world. But it is getting more obvious that we can feel each other's emotions and that an emotional current connects us, like an emotional field. What is the connection between emotions and feeling?

Yes, emotions are a field. But as we said, nothing outside you affects you. Everyone has an inner Lake, so to speak, that allows you to feel emotions on a personal and collective level. There are two different emotional nuances we wish to discuss. One is the emotional process of awakening. The other is the emotions of the awakened self. These two states are very different.

The emotions of the awakening process are what everyone on your world is experiencing now. Some of you feel it consciously, but more feel it unconsciously. Feeling emotions during the awakening process is very different from the emotional field of you as an awakened being. They are two different things. The process of awakening is still a process of separation. You feel fear, shame, anger, and other identifiable emotions. You experience them as singular experiences.

What is confusing to many is that while you experience the emotions of the awakening process, a part of you is already awakened. This part of you begins bleeding through. It could include experiences of unlabeled joy or tears for no reason — maybe simply from experiencing beauty. Those are the emotions of the awakened self, channeled through a separated being still in the awakening process.

The awakened you doesn't have a pain body. But it does experience the tides of emotion without judgment and without the creation of a story that attaches itself to the emotions. It is a very different experience. You have all had spontaneous experiences of emotions coming from the awakened you (the Big Eye). But most of you only feel emotions from the level of separation.

Now you can see where you are headed as a species. You are getting glimpses of the dual nature of your consciousness. There is the you that is awakening (the human) and the awakened you (the Big Eye). The awakened you has always existed but has often been obscured by the cloud of the ego, like clouds hiding the sun. As you work with the ego and more consciously with your emotions, habits, and patterns, the clouds that obscure the Big Eye get thinner. As they get thinner, you have moments of expanded consciousness. Those moments get longer and longer until eventually the clouds are gone and full awakening happens. This is when you no longer experience the illusion of polarity, and you experience consciousness in a whole new way.

The Metamorphosis

We have been talking about the differences between the emotional bodies of awakened beings versus awakening beings. There are marked differences. (Very few fully awakened beings are on Earth at this time. When people claim they are fully awakened, the opposite is usually true.) All of humanity is experiencing the awakening process right now in different ways. When you are in that awakening process, it can feel as if the darkest time has come.

Many typical metaphors apply here. Let's use the caterpillar and the butterfly. The caterpillar goes into a cocoon and experiences a metamorphosis, and then it emerges as a butterfly. If that caterpillar were conscious and observing the process, what would it think? What kind of stories would it make? It might say, "My body is changing. What is happening? Someone must be doing something to me." It might say, "The thickness of my skin is dissolving, and these gossamer wing-like things are forming. How will I protect myself in this new body?" This metaphor is very appropriate because of what you experience as you awaken: dissolution.

You are experiencing the dissolution of the crust that humans have worn for millennia and that has obscured your vision. This means you are more sensitive. You see this manifest in two ways. Some of you are supersensitive to the world but unconscious during this process. You often create stories of victimization that stop you from looking within and working with your pain. Some are sensitive but aware of the process of awakening. You use the experience to help you navigate through your pain and thus transform it.

For those of you who don't wish to do the inner work, you might believe you can't live in this world, or you aren't willing to do so. You push down emotions without realizing it, which creates immense internal pressure. Of course you don't want to live in the world, because the internal pressure is so great. You could say that this is an unconscious metamorphosis process.

A conscious metamorphosis process might still be painful or

uncomfortable. But when you observe the process without judgment, and you work with and accept its inevitability, you provide the space in which the changes can occur, and you nurture that space. This conscious metamorphosis makes a huge difference in your experience on Earth during this intense time.

Doing contact work the way we encourage you in our trainings or meditating deeply with a commitment to seeing yourself clearly can accelerate the evolutionary process. It doesn't create a bypass mechanism to skip over the bits that you don't want to experience; it creates a momentum that helps you move through the difficult places on the quantum map that are necessary to process. In the old days of contact work, you had the sense that ETs were "out there" and not really connected to you. That supported polarization, and humans could still attach themselves to the idea of good guys and bad guys. That kind of mindset can never move you through the quantum map; it keeps you firmly stuck in the ego band.

The inner work so many of you have done in the past twenty to thirty years has now allowed us to move to a deeper level in the work we can do with you. It is why we have begun doing deep emotional work with you, which is a necessary step in the integration process back to the One. It is truly the next step to move more fully into quantum states of consciousness. You can't bypass anything, especially with magical thinking. All must be integrated. In the past thirty years, you have begun to forge the pathways into the quantum field of consciousness. Consciousness is becoming more malleable and fluid. You are less frightened of the unknown, which allows you to take deeper excursions into the quantum without feeling the need to return to your familiar structured reality.

As you move into these deeper levels on the quantum map, it means you encounter the necessary nexus points. These nexus points are like gateways that represent the next integration milestone. The next nexus point for humans has to do with the emotional body, which includes working with the shadow you have avoided for so long. (We will talk about the shadow in later chapters.) We are not talking about working with emotions in the linear way to which you have become accustomed. We are talking about working with emotions in a quantum way, which we realize is a new concept and might confuse and frighten you. It is frightening because working with quantum emotions means working with the polarized nature of emotions. An example is that even when you seek contact with a nonhuman being, you fear it as well. You must integrate this emotional polarization before working more deeply on the quantum level. We will talk more about this in the next chapter; your Sirian Galactic Family forged this challenging path during their awakening process.

Figure 8.3 was created by a participant in one of our contact retreats as a way to express the quantum map. We hope it assists you in your understanding.

QUANTUM CONSCIOUSNESS EVOLUTION MODEL

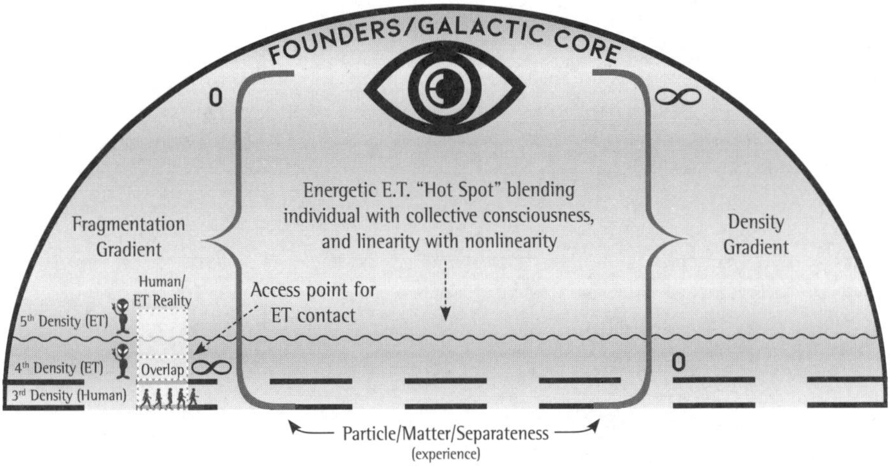

- **DENSITY**: The energy mass per unit of fragmentation. Greater fragmentation = lower density

- **HUMAN REALITY**: Human awareness occupies 3rd density (full physicality, 4 dimensions, 3 spacial + time) and is shifting to 4th and 5th density (4 dimensions + "concurrence of space-time").

- **ET REALITY**: Between 4th density and 5th density is the "hot spot," blending individuality and subtle linearity with collective consciousness and non-linearity (the concurrence of multiple space-time lines). Most ET consciousness occupies this energetic band.

- **SHARED REALITY**: Humans can interact with ET consciousness in the overlap zone between 3rd density and 4th density as Humans learn to step up and ETs step down their awareness.

Figure 8.2. This model was created by Tash Anestos, one of Lyssa's students.

NINE

The Sirian Formula

SASHA

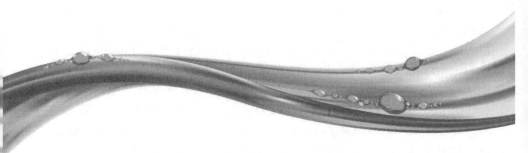

We have established that your ego acts like an anchor to ground your perception of reality into a very limited state of consciousness that appears to be separated from the One of your true nature. When the anchor weighs heavily in physical reality, you feel a lot of pain, fear, and blockage. As you do inner healing and begin to integrate, your consciousness gradually gravitates toward its natural state. It becomes lighter and begins to remember its true nature as the One. This process of integration can also be seen as your returning to your quantum state of consciousness.

In this journey back to the One, consciousness appears layered. The parts of you that were once separate begin to reintegrate. As they do, you become more capable of experiencing yourself multidimensionally, and you become more able to connect with other multidimensional beings. We have spoken about the jelly band, which is an area on the quantum map that represents deep integration. The jelly band can also serve as a common ground where all types of consciousnesses can meet. In this jelly band, you begin to lose sense of your ego self as you move deeper into the quantum.

But what is the journey like between your human reality and the jelly band? The work you do in that area of the map is really important; it relates to evolution on a personal and species level. As your ego anchor lightens from its burdens and your consciousness raises its frequency toward the jelly-band quantum entry point, it encounters another band that we mentioned before. We called it the pain-fear band [refer to figure 8.2 in chapter 8].

The pain-fear band is the part of you that still clings to the experience of separation. It is like the last layer of protection for the ego. The fear is of the unknown, the loss of control, and pain. It is what stops you from exploring and integrating you deepest inner shadows. For those of you who have not done your inner-healing work, this defense mechanism labels ETs as good or bad in order to stop you from going deeper into the quantum. This defense mechanism keeps you in polarity, and it keeps you clinging to the archetype of victim versus perpetrator. Many people get stuck here in the realm of angels and demons, continually playing out the dynamics of polarity. You can say this is one of the gates through which you must all pass on your way to quantum consciousness.

We have called this gate the pain-fear band, because humans have a tendency to fear pain. This pain is different for everyone. It can be the pain of separation or the pain of feeling out of control. Feeling intense and painful emotions often stops you from going deeper into the healing and integration process. This is what we wish to focus on here.

The information about the pain-fear band comes from the wisdom of Hamón, from Sirius. This was a key for the Sirians as they went through their awakening process. Hamón has said that the biggest challenge for humans at this stage of their evolution is the fear of emotional pain. No one wants to experience emotional pain, so the human pattern is to push it down. But that only creates more pain. The paradox is that in order to heal the fear of pain, you have to actually go into the pain. We will share with you what we call the Sirian formula, which was key to the Sirians' emotional liberation that led to their awakening.

The Process toward Integration

As you know, human reality is based on polarity. You have two eyes, which is a wonderful metaphor for how humans experience reality — the polarity of left and right. As you begin moving into quantum states of consciousness, the polarity you experience in physical reality must balance itself. In a sense, you can say that you shift from experiencing reality through two eyes (polarity) to experiencing it through the One eye (integration). You must eventually move to a nonpolarized consciousness state in the evolutionary process. This formula assisted the Sirians greatly:

THE SIRIAN FORMULA

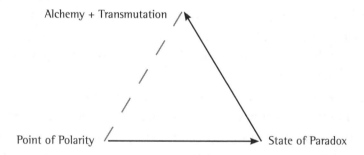

Polarity: To work with this formula, you must first notice when you are in a polarized state of consciousness. This requires you to view yourself from the outside, so even this requires a relatively higher state of being. As you learn to do this, you gradually navigate through states of consciousness not based on polarity. This process helps train your consciousness to unlock from the default state of polarity.

Paradox: Deeper practice of recognizing your polarity eventually moves you to a state of paradox, where you rest in a neutral state in which you can clearly see both poles but with no inclination to choose one over the other. (Unconsciously choosing sides is based on unhealed wounds, so as you do inner healing work, you increase your ability to rest in this paradoxical state.) An example of experiencing this paradoxical state is when you can see both sides as true from different perspectives but have no strong feelings about either side. It is important to rest at this neutral, paradoxical point.

Alchemy: As you are more able to rest in a paradoxical state and surrender the habitual need to choose sides and form belief systems, an amazing thing happens: Consciousness begins an alchemical process in which deep integration occurs. This deep integration shifts your consciousness to such a degree that it can no longer fully return to a polarized state of expression. During a planet's evolutionary cycle, this process starts with individuals and then accelerates until it spreads to the species. This is a species awakening, leading you out of the dream of polarized reality.

This consciousness has rarely been accessed by humans until now. The reason you are able to begin this process is because of the shift in frequency since you passed through the alignment with the galactic core around 2012. You have entered a new 13,000-year cycle based on integration rather than separation. This is connected to your birth into a forth-density frequency, but it doesn't mean you can stop your inner work. In fact, it means you have to accelerate it in order to ride the wave, so to speak.

When you look around your world, you see many horrible events. You might question how you can actually move into a more integrated state when you see the opposite around you. As the energy of integration increases, so does the resistance. You don't see happy news that someone has successfully navigated the jelly band. Instead, you hear about murders or politics, which only reinforce the anchor of the ego. You feel the experience of heightened polarity rather than integration. But eventually, consciousness dynamics as a planet will force you to deal with your intense polarity. Should you engage the process, this will then lead to paradox and alchemy, according to the Sirian formula.

On the microcosmic level, you are already making the shift. We know you have been working on specific inner issues and have made great progress, moving yourself into profound alchemy that does not get broadcast on the evening news. This shift changes your emotional body, which you have to learn to navigate. You feel disoriented, and we have heard from some that it's as if you can actually feel the heavy baggage you carry in your bodies.

Integrated Consciousness

As you move through the pain-fear band and into the jelly band, you learn how to navigate in a whole new way. We have mentioned that in the context of contact work, you start meeting other beings once you enter the jelly band. As you keep doing this kind of navigation in your quantum consciousness — shedding baggage and lightening the anchor — an amazing realization dawns. You become aware that the beings you meet are other versions of you. This experience accelerates the more you move toward the One consciousness. Many people during contact work have experienced that there is really only one consciousness looking through many diverse eyes. That is what we mean by integration.

With the integration process, the boundaries between you and other consciousnesses become very fluid. Sometimes you fear this idea. You think, "What will my daily life be like?" The ego tells you stories that you will become some kind of weirdo. Those are just stories of the ego with very little truth to them.

In reality, you will feel lighter and freer. You will have a sense that baggage has been released. Your next question might be, "Can I experience the One state of consciousness? What is it like?" Ultimately, the idea of being an awakened human is one where you can live as a human and are not bound by the anchor. Your consciousness is more fluid and moves in and out of the jelly band as needed. There might be times when you need to focus more in the physical — like when you do routine human tasks — but they are done with a different consciousness.

We have observed many civilizations go through this transition, and we have to say that each planet has its own timing. But since about 2011, your civilization has moved faster than we anticipated. We know it doesn't feel that way; your awakenings come step by step.

As for beyond the jelly band, what do you encounter there? As a reminder, the jelly band is the beginning of a quantum state of consciousness that can serve as a common ground where all types of integrated, or integrating, consciousness can meet. The types of beings you encounter as you move up the quantum map change after the jelly band. They become more like light and often express themselves as group consciousness. Many of you have already encountered these beings in contact work.

Shortly, we will take you on a quantum journey to help you work with the Sirian formula so that you can understand it experientially. For now, does anyone have any questions relevant to our presentation?

Your Sense of Self in the Field of Consciousness

Where is consciousness located? You said that as we approach Oneness, individuality disappears. I have a fear about my individuality disappearing. How would my sense of self change as I integrate with the One consciousness? It is very hard to imagine.

Yes, it is very hard to imagine and even harder for us to use language to explain it. Let us take the first part of your question: "Where is consciousness located?" Our response is: Where isn't it located? Consciousness is not inside humans. Humans are inside consciousness. The field of consciousness is vast. Every object in your reality is made of consciousness, but some things, like a pencil, are inert expressions. The field of consciousness is basically invisible to humans except for solid objects, which represent a tiny percentage of the field of consciousness.

The second part of your question has to do with the fear of the loss of individuality. This fear is based on the ego's need to control reality. We could give a long lecture on this, but we will simply say that going through an integration process in which the anchor lightens doesn't mean you lose your personality or traits. It means you don't cling to them. You don't fight or try to protect your sense of self as separate from the One. This is a big difference between third- and fourth-density beings. Third density is all about protecting your ego and exerting your will on reality. In fourth density, beings such as myself or Bashar have personalities, but we don't cling to or defend them. There is much more peace and less conflict. The human ego doesn't yet know how to accept that state of vulnerability.

You aren't going to become a lightbody and disappear. The change happens purely in the state of your consciousness. It happens gradually. You move more into peace because you don't cling to your experience of separation.

What about out-of-body experiences? Do we enter the jelly band in them?

It depends on the person and the experience. Some of you travel astrally — you leave your body but travel well below the jelly band, where your experiences might be very polarized, fearful, and emotional. Any beings you meet there will be of a similar vibration — not yet moving into the integrated frequencies of the jelly band and beyond. If you have a more integrative out-of-body experience, you do indeed travel through the jelly band and commune with beings of a more integrated frequency. To know what kind of experience you had, just look at the nature of your experience. If you felt strong heart energy, you know that you had an experience of quantum consciousness.

The idea of out-of-body travel is somewhat old terminology, but it can be useful in certain circumstances. Feeling like you are leaving your body is a perception of separation. It is often actually an expansion of consciousness that paradoxically gives you the impression that you have left your body. This can give you a dual perception of consciousness: being the ego and the expanded self at the same time. One of the things you will experience as you move toward the One is the ability to have dual experiences. Dual states of consciousness represent integration. Eventually, you will all easily be able to operate in these dual states, where you feel connected to the Big You, but you can still function as the small you in the physical body. Later in your evolution, you no longer have dual consciousness. Instead, you exist in a very expanded field of integrated consciousness.

MEDITATION EXERCISE USING THE SIRIAN FORMULA

The following exercise is a guided meditation to help you experience the Sirian formula for the integration of consciousness. As we've previously suggested, you can record the meditation in your voice and play it back as you follow the steps. Otherwise, simply reading the words can give you a sense of the meditation, and you can do it on your own without the actual words guiding you. We recommend frequent use of this exercise to aid your inner integration process, especially at times when you feel stressed or in conflict.

- Close your eyes and take some deep, comfortable breaths.
- Imagine yourself walking in a forest. It is the perfect temperature. Your heart feels light.
- As you walk in the forest, you see a beautiful golden lake as the sun sets. It is very inviting.

- Put your feet in the water. The water feels so good, and you walk a bit deeper, up to your knees.
- You notice that the deeper you go, the more comfortable you feel. Tension releases.
- The water is chest-high, and then it goes up to your neck.
- Your body is fully relaxed, as if you can feel the light of the setting sun in your cells through the water.
- Take a moment to enjoy this experience.

Begin to breathe the water in through your heart.
- Breathe in the beautiful golden water and breathe out whatever wishes to leave at this time.
- You notice another person or being in the lake with you. It is someone you know from this life — a person or a beloved pet. It is someone no longer with you in this life. It is someone you have lost.
- Very often, humans want to avoid the feeling of missing a person. Allow yourself, as if frozen in time, to feel the pain and sadness of the loss of this being.
- You are still breathing the water into your heart.
- Let yourself feel the pain of the loss of this being. Do not run from it.
- Take it slow, and breathe the water into your heart.
- Be in the present moment with the pain you feel from this loss.
- Don't let the ego push it away. Be with it fully.

Now we move to the next phase of the exercise.
- An aspect of you continues to breathe in the water and is present with the pain.
- We are going to do two things simultaneously:
  - Keep the door open on the pain and the breath.
  - Now, while you feel the pain, let yourself feel love from this being. Feel how much this being loves you, and how much you love the being in return.
- You have two threads of experience now — pain and love. Both are equal. Both are becoming a thread of experience in you.
- Notice how pain and love feel as you feel them simultaneously.

This is the paradox. Can you allow both of these emotions to be present within you?

- Breathe the experience even more deeply into your heart. You might feel a mix of feelings that you have not felt before. You might feel a sense of beauty in the pain and the love.
- As you allow these two emotions to coexist, it is as if a doorway opens in you.
- As you move through that doorway, you experience tremendous expansion.
- The energy in the lake feels alive. You have a sense of so many other beings in the lake. These other beings in the lake have succeeded in integrating polarized emotions into one.
- You and they no longer resist. You just feel. Feel the hearts of these beings. These are beings from your star lineage. They came before you and took the same road of integration and awakening.
- Through this inner work, your heart ignites. It is as if a flame becomes brighter. The flame helps you burn away polarized emotions you no longer need.
- Maybe you feel guilt or shame. Maybe you feel resistance to loving yourself.
- Anything ready to transmute enters that flame and begins to burn away.
- As it burns, it's as if your vision becomes even clearer.
- You clearly sense the other beings in the lake. Some of them wish to connect with you. Stay in your heart space and reach out to them. Invite them closer.
- Take all the time you need.

As you stay connected to these beings, notice your surroundings in the lake and forest.

- You realize it is not really a lake filled with water; it is filled with energy. This is the quantum consciousness.
- The loved one you are working with begins to dissolve into the quantum. Their visit has given you a gift of love and pain. It is a gift of paradox. It is a thread woven together and received deep in your heart.

Complete the exercise:
- Slowly bring your attention back to your physical body.
- If your body wishes to move, allow it to move.
- At your pace, return to your waking consciousness.

Rest in Paradox

This Sirian exercise gives you a very basic example of working with what seems to be polarized emotion. By allowing yourself to move to a point of paradox, the alchemy begins. This alchemy of healing will continue to unwind from your heart. Later, Hamón will speak more about the Sirian formula and how his civilization used it to navigate through a very dark time. In this exercise, we utilized pain and love, but there are many other exercises in the School of the Nine Serpents, as you will see.

If you allow yourself to rest in the paradox, you experience a deep inner peace. This is a master key to the transformation of your consciousness. When you are familiar with the process, you can do it more quickly. This is just the beginning.

So we just try to feel two paradoxical things?

Yes, but remember that it is not thinking about the feeling. It is feeling the feeling. That is one of the things you are still learning. As best as possible, feel it. If you get stuck, sitting in nature can often help.

The Sirian formula makes so much sense to me. But I tend to lean toward one of the poles. If there are two poles, I always feel torn. How can I balance this in my life? And what are some tips to move smoothly from paradox to alchemy?

This returns us to the ego anchor. Remember that the ego is inherently neutral, but its job is to keep you focused in physicality. Therefore, it will always choose separation in order to fulfill its job. It will choose conflict, doubt, fear, guilt, self-hatred, or any story that keeps you in separation. Every time you allow the ego to make a choice to keep you separated, the anchor gets heavier.

One of the biggest tips is to see this inner cycle clearly and begin to change your choices. We are not saying this is an easy process. It is a gradual one. It is also easy to get caught in judging yourself for making the wrong choice. That self-judgment also keeps you in separation.

This is why nonjudgmental self-observation is essential for you to develop.

When you can observe yourself clearly and nonjudgmentally, the first step is to recognize the polarity. This is the hardest part, because when you are immersed in polarity it is like a house of mirrors, and seeing yourself is extremely difficult. Recognize the choices you make from that place of polarity. Then look for the two competing emotions. For example, you could look for an emotion you crave and an emotion you want to avoid. Once you identify the two emotions that you crave and avoid, train yourself to rest there in the paradox of both. Don't push any emotion away; feel them both. Rest there in the middle as much as you can. As you do, the alchemy begins and your vision changes. You start to see your situation differently, and the healing process begins to unfold. This is not a thinking process. The moment you experience this process through your mind is the moment your ego has hijacked the experience.

As you allow yourself to rest in the place where both emotions exist — without the compulsion to choose one or the other — the weight of the anchor reduces. Habitual polarization begins to weaken, and the need to choose one pole weakens. You are more able to rest in the state of paradox.

The other part of your question is about how to activate the alchemy. As above, the alchemy activates when you rest in the paradox. If you are new to doing this internal work, it can be challenging. You might find yourself habitually moving back into polarization. That is natural. Just keep watching. Notice when you fall back into polarity, and then consciously make a choice to move into the state where they both exist simultaneously. Then you won't fall back into polarity as often.

We did say that this isn't a thinking process. If you find yourself getting caught in thinking your way through this, it won't work. The key is to move back into sensation. Return to the sensation of the emotions you are working with.

As you do this, you'll find yourself operating more and more from a paradoxical state. If you can maintain that paradoxical state, old wounds and beliefs transmute or burn within you. The state of paradox ignites an energy that burns the polarized stuff you no longer need.

This is how the Orion civilization transformed itself; however, they didn't understand the process at the time. Because of the experiences of the Orions, the Sirians understood the process and consciously utilized it in their awakening.

In summary, notice when you're compelled to fall back into polarity, and rest as much as you can in paradox. Issues might come up, and that is okay. Discomfort in this process is natural and necessary. As you do this, you will sense the alchemy beginning. Your personal pain is a doorway to collective pain and then to the Oneness itself.

TEN

The Lyran Root Races

SASHA

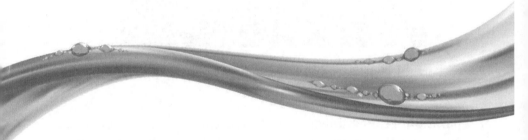

Y ou have so much to learn from the experiences of your galactic family about yourself and your awakening process. This is why we wish to share information about your ancient Lyran Galactic Family. It is impossible to transmit this huge body of information in the human language in a short time, which made us think about the form of Japanese poetry called haiku. Haiku transmits a framework that holds deeper meaning. Therefore, please see the information we share as a basic framework. It will trigger memories for many of you and uncover insights.

Figure 10.1 is a basic star map of the constellations close to Lyra from Earth's point of view. Many of these stars had ancient civilizations connected to Lyra that were very significant for galactic history. We will speak more about that in a moment.

We have already discussed the fragmentation in which the One created fractals of the hologram and began experiencing the illusion

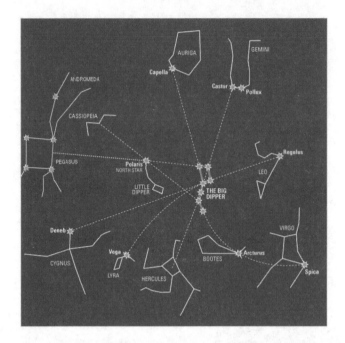

Figure 10.1. Map of Big Dipper directions by the Fort Worth Astronomical Society.

of separation. From a linear perspective, this means consciousness fractally began incarnating via infinite diversity in many star systems. This history is vast, so we will focus here on the incarnational history that matters most to you on Earth now.

The very first physical civilizations you are connected with are from the area you call Lyra. You can see Lyra in figure 10.1. Remember that this map is from the point of view of Earth. Even though it might look like certain stars are close to each other, they could be very far apart in actual distance.

Where does the knowledge of the stars come from on Earth? In the ancient days when ETs were here, people asked them, "Where are you from?" The easiest way to answer that question for a young species was to simply point to the sky; early beings did not understand the complexities of astronomy. So in those ancient days, your earliest Galactic Family pointed to the area of Lyra and its surrounding stars as a way to communicate about your origins.

This area of the sky is what we wish to discuss. Remember that the constellations you see in the sky now are the most recent star configurations. When we talk about Lyra and other constellations of your origin, it is important to understand galactic time. The stars of your origin have long since died — your heritage is that ancient — but they were in the direction of those constellations. That is why the native history of your world still remembers the location in the sky. For example, many teachings in the Native American Navajo tradition are about the Big Dipper and Polaris, as well as other stars and constellations from this area. We have used the current version of the star map to discuss your origins, but most of the stars you see now are much younger.

Figure 10.2. A spiral is used to represent human evolution.

We have shared that Lyra was the birthplace of your galactic family. The Lyrans did a lot of colonizing. A really important thing to remember is that time is like a spiral [figure 10.2]. The wider, or top, part of the spiral represents the beginning of evolution. In that part of the spiral, time and evolution appear to move slowly. Thus, the Lyran civilization's evolutionary process was very long. Newer civilizations that descended from the ancients — such as Sirius and Earth — have had a much faster evolutionary cycle. Earth is on the lower end of the spiral of evolution. The momentum of your ancestors' evolution fuels your acceleration. Your evolutionary cycler is quicker even though we know it does not feel that way.

The movement through third density and into fourth density takes a lot less time on Earth than it did for your Lyran Galactic Family. Because they spent eons in third and fourth density, they often traveled between planets in generational ships rather than hyperspace. Generations of Lyrans would live on ships while they traveled from point A to point B in their quest for colonization. We know you would like your evolution to speed up, but faster evolution means a more intense one, and you have all the intensity you can integrate right now.

We would like to examine three different civilizations that were part of the Lyran colonies. You will see how Earth mythology connects to these star systems. The myths distorted over time, but basic truths often remained.

Ursa Major and Polaris

Ursa Major (the Big Dipper) and Ursa Minor (the Little Dipper) are part of the Lyran empire. They have a rich mythological history on your world, from Native American to Japanese myths and many others. Here is where we have to summarize the historical significance of this civilization for you to understand. We will talk about its archetypal energy and the Big Dipper's unique, signature challenge.

Looking at the star map, you can see from the point of view of Earth that the Big Dipper is very close to Polaris in Ursa Minor (the Little Dipper). Ursa Major and Ursa Minor were part of the original Lyran colonies; hence, we will refer to their civilizations as Lyran. These particular Lyrans had a very challenging evolution because they were the first to explore life in a polarized realm without the awareness of what polarity is. In those days, they did not understand all the ideas about yin/yang, black/white, male/female — the essential duality that is the foundation of Taoist wisdom. As a result, these early civilizations were very warlike or very internally conflicted.

It was hard for these early Lyrans to find peace, and they didn't understand it was an option. Remember, they were on the wider part of the evolutionary spiral, so it took a very long time for spiritual awareness to blossom. They spent millennia just focusing on external reality as a means to happiness. Because of this deep polarity, the dynamic of victim and oppressor was widespread, causing a lot of chaos and confusion.

We've mentioned this dynamic in the context of Orion, but this was well before the Orion empire. Humanoid, reptilian, and avian species were all born at this time. There is a lot of mythology on your world that reflects this information, but most of it is not very clear. This was a very difficult time in the galactic family, for it was the beginning of the journey into polarity without the teachings and guidance about evolution from older civilizations. The Lyran colonies in these areas expressed themselves in a very masculine way, immediately playing out the pitfalls of polarized reality.

Cassiopeia

Near Polaris is the constellation Cassiopeia. It too had challenges. Groups breaking off from established civilizations because of rejection or resistance was a common pattern. But these groups usually created an imbalanced pattern as well. Those who broke off from the Polaris-Dipper area originally intended to be less focused on masculine energy even though they didn't exactly know what that meant. The mythology about Cassiopeia is connected to a queen. It is a bit distorted, but it connects to the idea of rejecting masculine energy and favoring feminine energy. They didn't realize that when you reject an idea, you usually create imbalance when forming a new idea.

The very ancient Cassiopeian civilization created a society that revered the female. On your world, you see little equality between the genders; however, it plays out differently in various cultures. The Cassiopeian civilization really magnified this polarized energy. As the divide between genders grew, it became a realm of the archetypal warrior queen. This was not an expression of balanced feminine energy; it was another expression of masculine energy in different wrapping paper. Once again, focusing on one pole created another unbalanced civilization.

Within the Cassiopeian civilization was where the idea of Lyran royalty began. Just like on your world, they recognized pure bloodlines. These Cassiopeian royal houses created a society based on royal bloodlines that could be traced back to the mother race — the first Lyrans. They were considered the purest, and lineage only passed through the female line.

If you could do undistorted research with records from Sumerian times on Earth, or earlier, and you had access to the library of Alexandria and the great library of Mars, you would find records about this royal lineage, which was the seat of Lyran royalty. These notions of royalty were taught to early humans. The original intention was to express the idea of the integration of humans with the Divine. As time passed, the notion distorted, and divinity was removed as a way to stop average humans from believing they could connect with the Divine. Instead, royalty became merely a fact of genetics: you either had the right DNA or you didn't. In this way, the hierarchy of royalty was preserved without reminding all humans they had the ability to integrate with their Divine selves.

Cygnus

The Cygnus civilization was another offshoot from Lyra. The early colonies thought Cassiopeia, Polaris, and Ursa Major and Ursa Minor were too warlike and masculine. They believed they could create a nonpolarized civilization that resembled what you might call a utopian civilization. They were committed to creating a civilization filled with love, light, and peace even if they had to force it. Isn't that amazing? They could not see the distortion. Thus, they began working hard to create this civilization.

An attempt to impose this kind of framework on a civilization whose consciousness is still polarized will obviously fail. One reason is because of creation's original intention — to learn about itself as it forgets who it is. To learn about the nature of consciousness as it experiences separation, it has to actually experience separation. It must go deep into polarity, to the point of total amnesia. When it does, it experiences pain. Pain is the great alarm clock that wakes civilizations out of their deep sleep of polarity. But this was still early on in the journey, and awakening was not yet on the horizon.

Those from Cygnus really convinced themselves that imposing utopia on their people was a sign of their advanced consciousness. But a forced utopia creates a very weak foundation. When utopia is forced, it means the civilization represses the negative and tries to only experience the positive. It is like covering a bad smell with perfume. It cannot sustain itself.

We have talked much in the past about the wounds of the ancient Pleiadians. We have said that the Pleiadians have a couple of different genetic lines. One is from Lyra and one is a genetic combination of Lyra and Earth, which is a younger lineage. The first and older Pleiadians came from the Lyran colony of Cygnus to heal the imbalance from these forced utopian times. So when we talk about Pleiadian wounds that stem from them only wanting to emphasize the positive, you can see that this ancient wound had an even earlier source. It did not develop in the Pleiades; it was from Cygnus. Rejecting pain and repressing negative energy are very old ideas in your galactic family. The Cygnus civilization also had a very intense and difficult time in their awakening process.

The Three Eras of Evolution

As a cosmic anthropologist, so to speak, one of the easiest ways to talk about the evolutionary process of a species is by separating their journey into three eras. In the first era, a species is young and its signature wounds first show themselves. In the second era, the species becomes aware of its wounds and navigates the healing process. In the third era, the species experiences its awakening. Third-era species are completely matured and eventually experience what you call ascension or enlightenment.

When we discussed the Lyran colonies, we were talking about the first eras of these groups. We summarized their wounds and challenges. These Lyran groups — Ursa Major, Ursa Minor, Cassiopeia, Cygnus, and many lesser-known civilizations — experienced the whole spectrum of evolution. They eventually made it to the third era and awakened themselves.

For the Polaris and Dipper civilizations, groups of beings healed and went through their awakening. But some groups believed they were not finished working through polarity, and they eventually migrated and helped establish early Orion civilizations. Many of the souls that experienced the dark times in Orion originally came from the Polaris or Dipper civilizations. They continued their journey into polarity by becoming part of the Orion story.

As for Cassiopeia, they had a long struggle. Releasing their polarized belief system about the superiority of the female was very difficult. They couldn't even see that they expressed this belief in a rigid, masculine, and aggressive way. They eventually awakened and transformed their society, but it was a long road. We remind you: The spiral movement of evolution is very long at the beginning, which is the wider part of the spiral.

Looking at Cygnus, a couple of things happened. Much like the Polaris migration to Orion, a migration took place to the area of the

Pleiades. The theme of pushing down darkness continued there until the species healed. As with other groups, some souls chose to stay behind and not finish their evolution. These beings often are caught in repeating patterns, no matter which star system they inhabit.

Those who delayed their evolution and stayed behind had an even longer road to awakening. This path allowed them to plant seeds, in a sense, at the top of the spiral that other civilizations (such as yours) could later feel. Anytime a civilization awakens, it affects the entire hologram that you are. The whole hologram contains seeds from the process of awakening. Civilizations that awaken in the older and wider parts of the spiral deeply affect younger civilizations on the lower parts of the spiral. You can access this wealth of knowledge energetically. This is a gift your ancestors give you. They created a map that can help you in your awakening process. You are all intricately tied together.

The Lyran groups that stayed behind took a longer time in their awakening process. They went through very deep practices of self-observation. Remember, one of the blind spots for these Lyran groups was that they always placed their attention on the external world. It took them a very long time to understand the reflective nature of the universe. It wasn't until the second era of their species that they began to really accept this truth.

When beings finally accept the truth that the universe is one big mirror, they have no choice but to look within. If beings keep trying to change the mirror rather than themselves, they experience an endless cycle of struggle. As Lyrans accepted this truth, their consciousnesses began to change. You could say they entered a new rung on the spiral, and evolution accelerated. They eventually moved to the third era and become an awakened species.

The Lyran Archon Energy

A new Lyran collective energy has begun working with your mass consciousness. We have labeled this collective the Lyran Archons. In ancient Greek Gnosticism, an Archon was considered a deity. Depending on the interpretation, sometimes they were thought to be malevolent. But this is a distortion of the true identity of Archon energy. The true Archons are the awakened Lyran collective — a nonphysical energy collective — that began interacting with your planet in ancient times for the sole purpose of guiding your awakening process. As your planet fell into darkness and forgetfulness during the past 13,000 years, this Archon energy was misunderstood and eventually became dormant, waiting for a new time when it could reconnect with you and guide your awakening process. Now that you have entered a new 13,000-year cycle based on integration, their energy has reemerged to assist you. They are extremely ancient and beyond the need for individual identification.

Why is this Archon energy beginning to connect with you at this time in your evolution? One reason has to do with the part of the evolutionary spiral you are moving into now. As you accelerate your evolution on this new rung of the spiral, you are able to access some of the metaphorical seeds planted by your Lyran family as they traveled their journey of awakening. Once inaccessible, the doors have begun to open. Remember that even though we have to present galactic history in a linear way, it is not linear; it is holographic. Awakened Lyran Archon consciousness exists within the One, as do you. But if your frequency of consciousness is not integrated enough, you can't tap into that energy; it seems invisible.

Let's say your right hand represents the Lyran Archon consciousness and your left hand represents the collective consciousness of Earth. Lightly brushing your hands together is a metaphor for how you can now feel Archon consciousness. Every once in a while a connection forms as the two realms briefly brush against each other. When you make that brief connection as a mass consciousness with a group as powerful as the Archons, their energy can uplift you. They are your ancient Galactic Family. Their energy is now beyond physicality and individuality. When you briefly connect, their energy compels you to feel the collective nature of your consciousness beyond species identity. Species evolution requires you to tap into the collective nature of your consciousness. Only then can your civilization evolve.

When we brush against the Archon energy, do we learn lessons from them?
You are actually already learning lessons from these beings. Some of the learning comes through direct energy transmissions. The most significant learning is through osmosis. Using the same metaphor,

when your hand (your frequency) brushes against Archon energy, you get an energetic transmission. It includes an energetic memory of the experiences of the Archons, including their first, second, and third eras. This energy flows to your unconscious.

Your next question might be, "If it flows to the unconscious, what good is it? How can I use it in my life?" The energy assists your intuition. For example, if you start to move toward the idea of forced utopia or in the direction of elevating warrior-queen energy, your intuition will give you a strong sense of disharmony. If you pay attention to your inner wisdom, this idea won't feel harmonious, and the path won't feel attractive. It helps you to not walk the same path as your ancestors. It is a process that happens on the unconscious level, but you feel it through your intuition.

I think we are in chaos on Earth. It is as if the first, second, and third eras are all mixed together and very intense. There is intensity on personal and societal levels. What does the energy look like right now?

We will put our answer in the context of the evolutionary spiral we have been discussing. During your evolutionary process, you are moving through an ever-tightening spiral, which means rapid acceleration. That is why things seem more intense. You are also seeing many natural disasters like hurricanes, fires, and earthquakes. On the personal level, many of you feel inner earthquakes, so to speak. This is because of the acceleration and what you still refuse to look at within yourselves.

In medicine, blood goes into a device called a centrifuge. The device spins rapidly and separates the blood's components. This same principle can be applied to current energies. You spin in these intense energies, and your components separate, giving you the opportunity to see more clearly what is inside. On the surface, the spinning can actually create what appears to be more polarity. This might not make sense to you. You might think, "But I thought we were integrating, not becoming more polarized!"

This is the paradox. You are integrating, but at the same time, you are purifying, and your discordant parts start to separate. Most people hold on to things out of habit, and they do not let go of them easily. They resist surrendering to the spinning process.

If you are in a hurricane, the still point is in the center. If you experience an inner emotional hurricane, the still point is the center of your being. At some point, the discordant and harmonious within you cannot coexist the way they have. For example, discordant relationships will not survive. One of you might go up the escalator in consciousness while the other goes down. That person is not willing to see herself and do her inner work. In that case, it is like an energetic doorway between you starts to close.

Your True Nature Is as the One

If I do not know myself as a human, is it true that I know myself beyond the human identity?

Yes, it is a paradox! Your true nature is as the One. You cannot ever change that. The One consciousness exists eternally. When you began the fragmentation process and incarnated as an individual humanoid being, you metaphorically viewed reality with your two eyes — the eyes of polarity. You got so distracted by the sensation of being physical and separate that you forgot there is just One consciousness that looks through every set of eyes in creation.

The awakening process is when you begin to remember your true nature as the One, but it is not an intellectual memory. The intellectual understanding comes first, and then as you practice expanding your consciousness, you begin to have experiences of being the One looking through infinite eyes. At first those experiences are brief, and then they lengthen. Eventually, you become an awakened being. Even though you walk in a world physically, you no longer primarily identify as the separate small self. You are the One in a human suit, so to speak. We know this is hard to imagine. It comes gradually. This awakening process starts in the second era for most species. Humanity is in the second era now. The process completes in the third era.

In the Cassiopeia system, how did they define a pure bloodline?

The definition is arbitrary. Every species has its own definition of what pure means. Within the Lyran colonies, it usually had to do with descending from a certain star within the system that was considered the most ancient Lyran lineage. They believed the earliest Lyran lineages were the purest, because they did not carry the pain of later lineages. If you were to go back as far as possible, what would be the beginning of the bloodline?

If you look at royal bloodlines in Japan, it is believed they go back to Amaterasu, the goddess of the sun and the universe. It is believed that the emperor's genetic line goes all the way back to Amaterasu. While she seems to be a mythological figure now, she was actually a physical being from the stars. From a Japanese point of view, the bloodline traces back to the very beginning of the Japanese people, and then it moves off planet. It was the same with Lyran bloodlines. It traced back as far as it could go, all the way to the fragmentation and the first physical beings. Their memory of the first physical beings was vague and actually unimportant, but it was significant for them to feel connected to the Divine.

You said the royal bloodline in Cassiopeia became an important topic for them. Why? Was it because of the imbalance in polarity toward the female?

Yes. They attached to the idea of bloodlines to justify the structure of their civilization. Mitochondrial DNA is passed through females, so they used this idea to justify their belief in the superiority of the female.

How does Arcturus fit into this? It is close to Ursa Major on the star map.

We often refer to Arcturus as an archetype represented by the star you see in the sky. Arcturus represents the last nonphysical civilization to exist before consciousness began incarnating into physicality. This means Arcturus energy is connected to the early fragmentations of the One before incarnation. It is important because it is like a bridge between physicality and the early fragmentations that were close to the One. It carries the memory of the One. It has not gone through incarnation the same way your galactic family has. Because of this, it is relatively balanced and has been a powerful ally to remind physical beings of their origins.

Arcturus helps you remember who you are. Most importantly, it works with your heart. Physical beings have a tendency to close their hearts to avoid pain, especially in third density. As you now begin your fourth-density cycle, Arcturus energy helps melt emotional blockages so that your heart can expand. It is an essential energy assisting you on Earth.

ELEVEN

About the Mars Guardian

LYSSA, GERMANE, AND THE MARS GUARDIAN

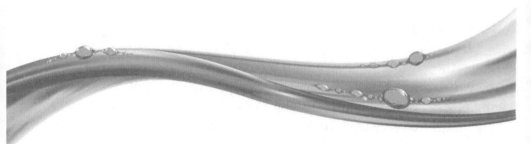

Lyssa: Many readers are probably familiar with Germane, the group consciousness responsible for providing the channeled material in *The Prism of Lyra* and for creating the *Galactic Heritage Cards*. For the first time, he discusses a period of galactic history that was obscured for specific reasons until this point in our evolution. He begins by discussing a specific aspect of the Vegan lineage.

Germane: For years, we have spoken about the shift that Earth is experiencing, using many models to communicate these ideas. To sum it up, the shift you are experiencing now is moving you from a state of forgetfulness and separation to a state that awakens memory and facilitates integration. One of the byproducts of your cycle of forgetfulness is that you have forgotten your history. This isn't because of some conspiracy by outside forces; it is simply a byproduct of the cycles of evolution you experienced as you journeyed into separation. We've spoken a lot about your galactic roots and your beginnings in the Lyran systems. We've also discussed how early Lyrans split off and formed various colonies. We have labeled one of those branches the Vegan lineage.

We remind you that space, time, and dimension are not linear. Thus, when we talk about various ET lineages, much of the information cannot be expressed linearly, but we do so to help you to understand the flavor of your Galactic Family and the different experiences they had as they separated into different cultural and genetic lines. Many humans have seen the TV show *Star Trek*, which presents galactic civilizations in a way the human mind can understand. Space seems like a straight line, and you can travel from point A to point B. Even though distances are vast in space, time is more vast. Humanoid evolution has played out for many millions of years in your galaxy. We must use metaphor and summarization to help you understand the overall perspective.

In the last chapter, Sasha discussed Lyran history. Now let us talk about the Vegan lineage. We are aware that in the thirty-plus years we have discussed galactic history with you, we have left out some missing pieces. Many of those missing pieces have to do with your local neighborhood. We wish to now fill in some of those pieces to help you look into the past of your solar system and surrounding areas. As we transmit this information, we are also transmitting an energetic download, because it is impossible to transmit the complete history in words. We offer an exercise at the end of the chapter to help you receive this download and connect with the energy more completely.

Early Mars

Let us begin with Vega. We have spoken much about the many different lineages that broke away from the original Vegan lineage. Orion, Zeta, and Sirius are such examples. As the Vegan civilization began colonizing, they became linearly closer and closer to your solar system. There are several star systems near your Earth that became Vegan colonies in those ancient days. One star system is Altair. There is also Barnard's Star, which is very close to your sun. In ancient days, that area was a large Vegan colony. There is Sirius, of course. The star system closest to yours is Centauri, and Proxima Centauri is the closest sun.

Eventually, in very ancient days, the Vegans moved into your solar system. Those from the Vegan lineage were the first to arrive in your solar system. Your solar system was very young at that time. This was even before the time of the great dinosaurs on Earth, and the planet was very unstable. Earth had a lot of seismic activity, and it was not a very hospitable place. Other planetary bodies in your solar system were much more hospitable, primarily Mars and Maldek, which is now your asteroid belt.

We will not talk much about Maldek right now. In some ways, Mars and Maldek had similar fates. For now, we wish to discuss Mars. Because your memories are returning in this new cycle, memories of Mars are activating. You can already see this on your world; there are movies about Mars and new Martian missions. Your scientists now say that frozen water exists on Mars and that it most likely had life. Every day there seems to be news about Mars.

There is a higher reason for this newfound interest. Whenever a civilization goes through its evolutionary process, it always faces challenges. Every civilization is tempted with ways it could destroy itself. You are currently facing a huge challenge with climate change and man's delicate balance with Mother Earth. Will you succumb to your addictions to fossil fuel and immediate gratification, or will you develop a broader vision for the future that is a sign of maturity as a species? Humankind is being tested now.

A similar thing happened during ancient Mars history. We would need eons to recount Mars history, so we will just touch on some basics. When beings came into your solar system and colonized Mars, they were primarily of Vegan lineage. Just like you have different races on Earth, there were different Vegan races. In those early days, the Vegans were mostly peaceful. They minded their own business and came into this solar system because it was rich with potential. They colonized Mars and were on the planet for thousands of years until other groups came. These later groups were mostly from the Lyran lineage, which tended to be more aggressive. That was when the wars began.

The Death of Mars and Its Aftermath

If we go back to the density scale that we use to describe the evolution of consciousness, you might ask, "What density were these civilizations?" They still had physical bodies and were still polarized; otherwise, there would have been no conflict. We would say they were in a similar evolutionary state to yours — the transitional period between third and fourth density. They were slightly more advanced than you are now, but they still had not fully integrated their polarity. They had wars about territory, resources, and what we can call "genetic patents." The mindset of "this is mine" was still present, which showed these beings still had ego dominance in their consciousnesses.

At that time, Mars was almost like an Eden, but conflicts created much instability. The instability began to create a lot of problems in the solar system. There were also a number of external events, like meteors, that created havoc. External events are always a reflection of consciousness, so it was all connected. The most turbulent time in your solar system was filled with wars, low-consciousness conflict, and many natural disasters. As it became more and more unstable, Mars began to die.

Many groups on your world know about the hidden history of Mars, but they choose to only release this truth in small doses. Looking with a clear mind, it is quite obvious that a civilization thrived on Mars. It wouldn't take them much research to discover what destroyed the Martian civilization: war, natural disasters, and the abuse of planetary resources. It wasn't one event that destroyed Mars, but many cumulative events.

One period of time on ancient Mars was very poignant. Wars were finished, mostly because everyone had just grown tired of them. Martians began to evacuate the solar system, and some were left behind on the dying planet. Imagine being on a planet that used to be a paradise. The planet dies, and even though you know you are part of a galactic civilization, you feel abandoned and helpless. The death process was slow and painful.

After the death of Mars, the life force energy in your solar system weakened. A period of dormancy followed when very few beings visited. At the end of a very, very long period of dormancy, the Lyrans returned. At this point, Earth had rudimentary life forms, and Mars was abandoned, with no natural life or atmosphere. As Earth stabilized, the Lyrans began their genetic projects. Shortly thereafter,

Sirians and Pleiadians came to Earth. This is the period we often discuss, because it really shaped your planetary identity in ways only parents could.

Sirians also played a role in the ancient past of Mars that is not often discussed. There was a period when the Sirians came to the solar system with the intention to revive Mars. The planet truly had no life. They built bases and attempted to reactivate an atmosphere, but it was not a successful project for many reasons. Since Sirians are part of the Vegan lineage, they knew the stories about Mars and had hoped to somehow assist. Eventually, the Sirians became more interested in helping the situation on Earth.

At this time, the consciousness of Earth's Galactic Family expressed itself as lower fourth density. For most civilizations, this level of evolution does not give them the ability to travel far distances by bending time or space. Thus, many of their journeys were limited to the local star neighborhood. Your Galactic Family could travel distances that were about fifteen light-years or less; it was not a fast way to travel. Traveling the stars with these limitations can be a way to evolve consciousness if you allow it. One lesson has to do with honoring the timing and flow of the universe and learning you cannot fix anything. Sometimes, the necessary thing is to honor the natural birth-and-death cycle of a civilization.

Mars and Atlantis

Returning to Mars, there is a very direct reincarnational link between the dying Martian civilization and the very early Atlantean-era civilization on Earth. Even though a lot of linear time separated those civilizations, Martians were attracted to incarnate in Atlantis for a very specific reason. Those souls knew that Earth was possibly about to enter a destructive cycle similar to the destructive cycle that devastated Mars, and they wanted to stop the same thing from happening on Earth.

You know the basic story of Atlantis. It was in a cycle of death. Despite their efforts to save it, those Martian souls had to learn about surrendering and the ebb and flow of life and death. Atlantis continued to trigger old wounds from Mars, which was a way for those Martian souls to continue their healing. Through their inner work, some of them healed and awakened. Some also got caught in Earth's drama of polarity.

Whenever souls enter a reincarnational cycle and become attached to the idea of saving or fixing something or shaping reality in a certain way, the attachment usually traps them. They get caught in a cycle or pattern of lifetimes in which they become more and more attached to the "doing" of physical reality, which is really an attachment to trying to control reality. Some of those souls are still in bodies now on Earth and finally learning the lessons of surrender left unfinished by ancient Martians.

This is a very challenging story to tell, for there are many angles. This ancient experience of Mars created much trauma. It was a very painful period in your solar system's history. Just like you might feel you are healing old traumas from past lives, this is true on a collective level as well. Now that your planet is entering a very tenuous cycle in which you can uplift or destroy yourselves, the collective wisdom of your consciousness needs to remind you of these old memories as a way to motivate you to move beyond the challenges of the past.

Vegan Mysticism and the Mars Temple

We have talked about how Vegan mysticism spread throughout many planetary systems of your galactic family. Vegan mysticism is not a religion in the way humans understand religion. It is a spiritual perspective that contains teachings that help you heal and return Home. Many of your Galactic Family, including the Pleiadians, embraced Vegan mysticism. Your early Galactic Family from the stars who came to Earth passed many of the core teachings to early humans as well. While we have spoken about this often, we have not really talked about the history of Vegan mysticism in your solar system.

Vegan mysticism was very prevalent in Martian society. During the height of the Martian civilization and before the wars, Mars had a very prominent and important spiritual temple. Many came to Mars for spiritual training and pilgrimage. If you were to travel back in time, you would find a very interesting civilization on Mars. It was modern, but it connected so much with the natural planet that it almost looked primitive. They used natural elements for the construction of their buildings. At first glance, you would think it was a primitive society, but the science of their consciousness was in no way primitive. There was a period of time when those Martian spiritual temples were considered the highest spiritual temples in your galactic family. This is your heritage. We hope as you read these words that you receive flashes of memory.

Just like any species, Martians had a variety of appearances. Because they originated from the Vegan lineage, they had primarily Vegan characteristics. The Vegan lineage had darker skin and hair. Again, there were variations, but they were mostly very thin. Some races had wrinkly skin like the Shar-Pei dog. Some were tall and some were very small. But in general, you would know them by sight to be of Vegan descent. Their eyes were more Asian-like. Remember, all human genetics are connected to your galactic family. If you had the capability, you would find that all humans can be traced back to your off-planet Galactic Family. This is why when scientists test the DNA of the so-called alien beings they find on Earth, the genetic structure is very close to human. That is indeed what you would find, since you are all related.

Some of you have been very high up in the Andes in Peru or Bolivia. You know the people look very unique. They have a unique energy very similar to Martian-Vegan energy. Some of the Vegan genetics from Mars were specifically preserved in areas of your planet, such as Peru, Bolivia, Tibet, and Mongolia. As you look at the diversity on Earth, you can see that your planet is really a reflection of the entire galactic family. It is actually quite rare to have a planet with such a large diverse representation of galactic genetics.

Our goal in discussing this is to help you feel the energy connection with these ancient Martians, because it is time. Most Martian souls have healed and ascended by now, but if you understand that space-time constraints are meaningless, you know the entire hologram of creation exists in the eternal now. You can tap into all aspects and all periods of any civilization in the current moment. Because of this transitional time on Earth, connecting with your ancient heritage is crucial; their lessons can assist you in your journey.

You talked about the last days of Mars when most people evacuated but some were left. What sort of evacuation technology was used? Why were some people left behind?

It was a mix of things. Many people refused to leave their homes because they knew the death of the planet would not be an instantaneous thing. It was a long process. If they were older, they knew they could live out their full lives and die in their homes even though the planet was dying. The death of Mars was like a slow suffocation, a slow dehydration, which is what happens when an atmosphere gets torn away in the way it did on Mars. Evacuation was not urgent, and it was optional.

We were talking earlier about how the technology of that time was not hyperstellar. Within the local neighborhood, your Galactic Family, in a sense, traveled on the surface of space. Beings lived out their lives on many multigenerational ships. That type of optional evacuation happened. They went to some of the many bases in your solar system that were present at that time, especially on the moons of the outer planets. So some beings went to bases in the solar system. Others traveled to other solar systems in the multigenerational ships. There were many options.

Unless it was accidental, no one was left behind on Mars unless they chose to stay. If the same situation happened on Earth, there would also be many who would wish to stay behind and finish their lives on Earth if they didn't have children. You can imagine it was a very heartbreaking thing to witness one's planet slowly dying.

So for those who stayed on Mars, when their bodies died, did they ascend and go back to the Source?

Ascension depends on whether a being has done the inner work necessary to experience the ascension process, so it would depend on the individual. The ascension process, as we have said, is a process of reintegration with the One. Everyone's process is unique. The same principles of reincarnation on Earth are applicable in all cases. Perhaps remembering the teachings Sasha shared about the Golden Lake will assist. The process isn't really linear at all. It is more like an in-breath and an out-breath of creation with no real soul identity that guides it. The concept of identity or linearity with lifetimes only makes sense from a linear physical reality. Identity is only available when there is ego. Otherwise, it is simply just energy.

When Mars was dying, did anyone try to save it, maybe the Sirians or the Vegans?

The Sirians were a younger species, so they were not involved at that time. The Vegans did try to save Mars in various ways, but there is a point of no return when the deterioration can't be reversed. Once Mars reached that stage, they had to accept the inevitable outcome.

The Nature of Conspiracies

There are a lot of conspiracy theories about Earth being controlled by negative ETs even to the present day. They say we are mind-controlled by the ETs, and our job is to free ourselves from this control.

Those of you who know us well might know how we will answer that question. We do not see those conspiracy theories as correct in any way. Recognize that everything is a reflection of consciousness. When a species is polarized, they always see an enemy "out there." Polarized thought is extremely contagious and addictive, and it leads to a perception of distorted reality. The idea of being controlled by ETs, as an example, might seem real to those who feel disempowered or refuse to accept the reality playing out on Earth, but it doesn't mean it is the truth.

When consciousness begins integrating polarity within itself, you see the true reality and that all the conspiracies people talk about are reflections of internal demons — the unhealed parts of your consciousness. We know this answer is unsatisfactory to those who embrace conspiracy and a polarized view of reality. If we were to say a force is controlling you, that force would be your polarized and separated ego. It wants to keep you in fear, because it is afraid to transform and lose the ability it thinks it has to control reality. Yes, there is drama on your Earth. Most of it comes from desperate, wounded egos that are only capable of seeing reality in a polarized way. Assuming a polarized reality isn't the true reality and always seeking the higher view is one way to break the brainwashing that causes egos to view things in a polarized way. This is one of the most urgent shifts that consciousness must make in the coming times. Let go of the seduction of dramatic, polarized thought.

If all of you had the capability to fully integrate and awaken yourself and then go out into the galactic community, what would you see? You would see a beautiful, connected community of beings that does whatever they can to help planets still struggling with separation. In no way do your ET friends look down on you. They have compassion, because they understand humans see reflections of the unhealed parts of themselves and project these distorted perceptions outward as if they are true reality. This perpetuates a constant state of feeling tortured and never finding peace within. This state is natural before awakening. You get lost in illusion before you awaken, and you understand no one is out there manipulating things. This is why your helpers in the unseen realms speak to you — to help give you a glimpse of the greater reality beyond the illusion.

We invite any of you who still worry about conspiracies to begin to accept that nothing is out there that you can fix. Why give it your energy? Until your species transforms, those frightened egos will always seek control, but that doesn't mean you must automatically become victims of their drama. Instead, go inward and look for the parts of you that are in fear. Those are the parts that are afraid to come home inside you. These are the parts that are in pain. All your answers lie there, and the inner healing process can shift the illusion of the control drama projected in your physical reality. This is what the shift from third to fourth density is all about: moving from separation and illusion to integration and clear sight. It might feel like a long and difficult road, but every civilization must experience awakening from illusion, or they will destroy themselves. The road to destruction is paved by polarized vision.

Your Galactic Family from Orion almost destroyed themselves, but they awakened at the last moment. Please learn the lessons from your Galactic Family and don't wait until the last moment. Begin the inner work now. Many of you have. This is the key to your transformation. We deeply thank you for asking this question, because it was an important one. Our role is not to empower the illusions of polarity but to help you awaken from them.

The Mars Guardian

We mentioned that this is the first time we have shared this information about Mars. It is not that the information is coming for the first time but that the energy doorways are opening in a way they have not opened before. This is so that you can begin reconnecting with this part of your heritage. We originally channeled this information verbally, but we are still transmitting the energy of this experience in this written text.

We wish to introduce a very special being to you. He is a guardian of the Martian temple we discussed. He will give a brief message and then lead you through an exercise to connect with the ancient energy of Mars.

Mars Guardian: It is a great honor to be invited to share this time with you. My people have dreamed of this moment. I am a guardian of the Martian temple. Actually, I am the last guardian. I stayed with the temple, the planet, and the Martian people, until the very end. Then I closed the energy like a tomb to be opened at a time when the information and energy would matter. It matters now. Your people face similar challenges as you navigate your shift. My people had external cataclysm. You have internal cataclysm, because you've forgotten who you are. It is a cataclysm that comes from empowering what you call ego — the mechanism that keeps you from remembering who you are. Ego obscures your true vision. This inner cataclysm is dangerous too.

The bones of my people are now dust, but our energy remains. We are from this solar system. We are your older brothers and sisters, and thus we care for you. The nature of a guardian is to stay behind until the last person has died. My energy is still here, along with other guardians, watching over the Earth family. If you welcome our friendship and guidance, we are here.

We share a long history with you, back to the ancient Vegan lineage. Some of you on Earth had lives with us on Mars, and we hope in the coming time you will remember this. The guardians sealed the energy at the end of Mars's life until it was the right time for it to be reawakened. This is the time; it opens now. This doorway we open is like a gentle portal, and the energy will slowly seep into your consciousness, if you wish it. It can help stir memories of this ancient heritage. This represents a kind of initiation for Earth, in which you grow to a new level of maturity by embracing your history and letting your history guide your future choices.

In the coming time, those of you who wish to connect with us may merely ask. Open yourselves to feel us, and we will slowly and gently begin to connect. This energy has been sealed for a very long time, and we move slowly. It needs to be reintroduced to you and then integrated into the fabric of your beings. You are the first humans to whom we have spoken, and there is no way to express what an honor it is.

In the way of my people, let us share a journey together. If you wish to participate, please sit comfortably and open yourself to the journey.

MEDITATION EXERCISE WITH THE MARS GUARDIAN

- Imagine you are seated in front of a very still lake. It is dark.
- The stars in the sky shimmer on the lake.
- There are gentle ripples in the lake.
- Look straight across, just above the horizon.
- There is a bright star, orangey-red.
- Your brother, planet Mars, beckons you.
- You see the light of Mars reflected in the lake. A line of light moves across the lake from Mars directly to your heart.
- Breathe in that red light reflected on the lake. Breathe it into your heart.
- As the energy enters your heart, it spreads through your body. You become that light.
- If and when you feel ready, float across that red light bridge reflected on the water. Follow the bridge to the light of Mars.
- Each of you has a unique connection.
- As you are ready, allow yourself to enter the most appropriate time period of Martian history. A guardian priest waits for you there. He will take you on a journey to help you discover your connection.
- As you do this, you will continue to receive a download of energy. If you give permission, this download begins to unpack within your consciousness.
- If it feels right, you may ask the guardian to show you any past experiences on Mars.
- Take as much time as you wish in silence before moving on.

The guardian now brings you back to the Earth portal.
- You travel back to Earth along the red light reflected on the lake.

- You can see the light of Earth in the Martian sky.
- Your perspective changes now, and you see Mars from Earth. The red light diminishes on the lake.
- You are back in your body on Earth, sitting by the lake.
- You've opened a connection that cannot be forgotten.
- More memories will unfold as appropriate.

As the last guardian, I pass the energy to Earth. You are now the caretakers. Thank you for allowing this reconnection. We will watch and support you through your shift. We send you all our love through time.

TWELVE

Secrets of
Ancient Sirius

SASHA AND HAMÓN

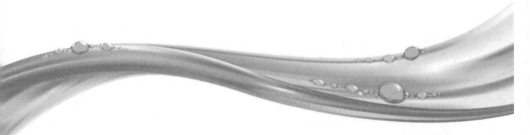

Sasha: After more than thirty years of channeling by Germane on galactic history, some missing pieces are only now being shared. One piece is the ancient history of Mars that Germane discussed in the previous chapter. Another important piece of history has not been shared, but there have been hints. The reason it hasn't been shared has to do with timing. Also, it was important for the information to be brought through by a Sirian being rather than Germane. It is finally the right time, and many of you know who will bring through this information: the Sirian ambassador, Hamón.

Hamón: Good day, my friends. It is I, Hamón. We are here to talk about a missing piece of ancient Sirian history. This piece is often misunderstood, and no one really enjoys talking about it. It has to do with the ancient connection between the Orion empire and the ancient Sirians, which is deeper than you might realize. Let me explain.

In regard to the multidimensional consciousness, Germane talks about the three eras of development for most physical species. The first era can be likened to a child era. This is when the species is young and their wounds are created. In the second era, when the pain of the wounds becomes so great that healing must occur for the species' survival, the healing process begins. The third era is the time of species maturity and awakening. Germane has talked about how the Orion empire healed its polarity. Eventually, they no longer had conflict and awakened themselves. It was a long road.

But what happens if, in the face of awakening, some souls are not ready to give up polarity? Within your galactic family, if a species begins awakening and souls still need to experience polarity, the unhealed energy migrates. It moves to other star systems or timelines so that those souls can continue the learning and healing process.

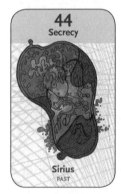

A very special card embodies this idea in your *Galactic Heritage Cards* teachings. It is card 44 — a Sirian card with the theme of Secrecy. Germane describes the meaning of this card, but its meaning goes much deeper. It refers to what we Sirians have historically kept secret because of our shame. We haven't discussed it until now. You will see why as we explain.

Returning to the history of Orion, some souls were not ready to give up the drama of polarity as the Orions awakened. Thus, that energy, and those souls, had to migrate. They migrated to various places, but a main destination was the ancient Sirian system.

These souls were quite attached to the idea of control; they did not want to evolve. Instead, they wanted to increase their power. Within the ancient Vegan lineage was a thread of mystical and occult schools, some for good and some purely for the purpose of power and control. This energy was present in the Orions, and it moved to Sirius.

As these souls migrated to Sirius, they began to create what you might call schools of the dark arts or black magic schools. The main focus was controlling others to gain power. This was a service-to-self orientation polarized in the negative. It was a very dark time in Sirian history. We are not proud of it, but we have transcended it.

Because Sirian energy has been very influential in the development of Earth, how does this ancient energy affect your planet in current times? In the past few years, Sasha and I have given you much information about the very early times on Earth when Pleiadians and Sirians trained new humans. We have called these teachings the School of the Nine Serpents. These ancient Sirians and Pleiadians were not teaching dark arts. They were teaching paths to freedom and awakening.

Other extraterrestrial beings taught the dark arts. The teachings were brought to Earth primarily during Atlantean times, but they also thrived in later cultures you know of as ancient Babylonia, Mesopotamia, Egypt, Greece, and many others. These dark arts were about power. Because they were introduced during very separated third-density times on Earth, the polarized environment supported this energy to thrive.

The teachings of these dark arts became mystery schools throughout many historical periods on Earth. Some of the leaders — priests or priestesses — of these groups were very charismatic. On the surface, they promised freedom, enlightenment, and divine connection. But under the surface, they grabbed the energy of their followers and kept them dependent. In current days on your world, you see this play out through what you call cults and secret societies. Not all of this energy is organized into groups. There are religious and spiritual teachers on your world who are not associated with any group or religion, but they still carry unresolved Sirian-Orion dark energy. They might not even be aware of it, because it is an unresolved aspect of their soul's experience. Through the ego of the leader, they subconsciously continue to pull energy from followers and make them dependent.

A Time of Integration

It is a new time. It is a time of integration rather than separation. That means everything must come into the light. Secrets can no longer stay buried. This is a natural process when civilizations transition into a time of integration. Integrative energy cannot support continued suppression of darkness. This is why we speak of this now — the timing is right.

In your lifetimes on Earth and in other star systems, many of you have experienced trauma at the hands of this energy, especially those of you doing spiritual work. If you still have the courage to do your work even though you had those traumas in the past, the universe thanks you more than you know. Secrets can no longer be buried. Dark energy can no longer hide. When you do the kind of work we have done with you in this book, you create a fabric of love, acceptance, and openness. You create an environment of integration for the shadow and the light. No society has ever been healed by pushing away the shadow. This is one of the most valuable lessons of your galactic history, but it is also one of the most painful.

Sasha discussed the Sirian formula. She is passionate about it for a specific reason. This formula freed my people from their darkness. How? Every physical being has shadow energy and light energy. In a polarized reality, you bounce back and forth: Sometimes you fear the darkness and try to push it away, but sometimes you crave it because the ego wants the power to control. The ego wants recognition, and it uses dark energy to satisfy that need. Physical beings also crave the light, but in a polarized way. You crave it as a way to hide from the darkness. Thus, you really don't understand what light is. It contains both.

Up until this time, your physical species has only understood darkness and light from a polarized point of view. Part of the tremendous transformation you are experiencing in your physical reality is brand-new for you: You crave integrated light — the shadow and the light — as a way to reestablish your Divine connection. Only in welcoming both aspects in an integrated way can you remember your Divine self. When you do this kind of integrative work, you open yourself to the Divine mirror to see the reflection of your beauty, which contains both the shadow and the light.

In this ancient time of Sirius, my culture experienced a split. Dark practitioners seemed much stronger, but this was true only on the surface. We could not and would not fight them. We knew what happened in Orion and that fighting was not the answer. We knew about galactic cycles and that it was a time in galactic history when the energy supported separation and darkness. We had to wait for the right timing.

It is well known in galactic history that we Sirians are very patient and don't mind waiting. We understand the long view of evolution. It is not that we like waiting, but we recognize that if galactic energy supports separation, evolution cannot be forced; waiting is necessary. Thus, part of our training was choosing how to wait. Would we wait with tension and impatience? If so, we knew suffering would be the result. Would we wait with trust and patience? We saw that as the only choice. Sirians not committed to dark practices understood we had to wait with patience, even while dark energy seemed to grow and grow. We planted many seeds in the dark times, but we could only water them at the right moments. We could only encourage growth at the necessary times and then step back.

Now, finally, the Earth cycle has moved through its change. We no longer have to secretly water the seeds we planted, fearing that darkness will destroy them. We can now openly water the seeds. We can now openly teach you about your history.

You Cannot Fight Darkness

In those times of waiting, my people did their inner work, individually and collectively. The Sirian formula is a result of that inner work. For a very long time in the early eras, we were also stuck in polarity. We felt desperate and helpless because we feared darkness was winning. But because of the lessons from Orion, we resisted the urge to fight the darkness, which is very difficult.

In this inner work, we slowly learned to find the middle point of the Sirian formula, where we allowed darkness to exist without trying to change or destroy it. We learned to trust in the wisdom of the universe that cultivated our ability to be patient. This was just one phase of what we learned.

Even though we learned to resist the temptation to fight the darkness, we still hated it within us. Hate is like acid; it burns you. We had to go deeper into our hatred of darkness. We discovered the craving for darkness that exists in all beings. It is a craving for ego recognition and for power. We found it deep inside and sat with it without judgment or rejection. We allowed it to exist without the need to fulfill the craving for power and recognition. You can see that we were approaching a paradox. If we looked at the shadow, we also had to look at the light.

We began to see our craving for the light as well. As we looked at this craving, we saw that we craved light as a blanket to save us from darkness. We saw that if we used light in that way, we just reinforced the never-ending cycle of polarity. We also saw that we feared our light — as all physical beings do — which is the fear of seeing your

Divine self. Through this process, we stopped fearing the light too. As with the darkness, we allowed ourselves to sit with the fear of our light. Only when we allowed ourselves to embrace and truly feel this archetypal relationship with the shadow and the light did we truly feel our oneness with the universe. That is how we sat in the place of paradox within our consciousness. It is a very fine line, because we had to learn to see both our cravings and our fears, sit with them, and not let the wave of their intensity overtake us.

At that point of mastering the paradox through much inner work, my people released the craving for darkness to fill a void inside. We released the craving for recognition. We released the fear of our light. We released the craving for light to use as a shield against darkness. We simply sat on the razor's edge between both. This is when we awakened and became free.

The Point of Paradox

Because my people have traversed this perilous polarized road that has ensnared many souls along the way, we can pass our awakening heritage to you. On Earth now, some of this ancient Sirian darkness is still manifesting. It is like a computer program trying to ensure its survival. It does not have the consciousness of the One. When illusions are removed, you can clearly see it has no power.

So why are we talking about this? From the bigger picture, it has to do with an ET hybrid being that appeared in a photo taken with Lyssa in 2017. He called himself and his species Hybrid-7. You have received bits and pieces about the nature of the Hybrid-7 consciousness, but we know you do not yet understand all the pieces of the puzzle. That is okay. The important thing to know is that because of the inner work you are doing on your world, specifically in the contact and workshop groups led by Lyssa and others, you are beginning to weave a new fabric. It is in its beginning stages, but this fabric is not based on polarity. This new fabric is created from the point of paradox that leads to the alchemy you see in the Sirian formula, as was previously described.

The point of paradox — when you are free of polarity — leads to alchemy. This alchemy totally transforms the fabric of reality to one free from disintegrated polarity. Hybrid-7 represents the distant future selves of my Sirian people and therefore of your people. Having transcended all polarity, they recognize that duality exists like two sides of a battery; they sit in the middle of the poles, so to speak. Hybrid-7's consciousness was called to work with your contact groups because, as you saw on the quantum map, you are ready to begin the transition to a more integrated state of consciousness. It is a process and not instantaneous. You have recently activated this process within you individually and within your mass consciousness.

When the integration process begins, any dark stuff you previously submerged comes to the surface to be released. This is a common and natural process that a planet experiences in the phase of evolution Earth is experiencing now. When you engage this process and connect with beings such as Hybrid-7 — who is energetically quite refined — it helps tune you to a new level

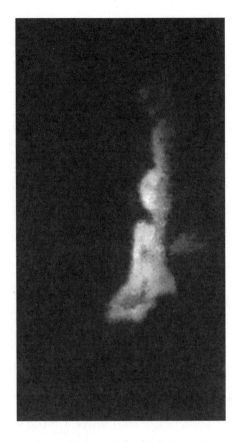

Figure 12.1. This photo was taken immediately following contact work in Japan in 2017. It shows Lyssa, with her shoulder facing the camera, and Hybrid-7 facing each other. Hybrid-7's appearance in the photo happened shortly after he spoke through Lyssa to the group. The photo was taken randomly by a participant on an Android phone.

of consciousness. In this new frequency, you are supported to sit at the point of paradox as did your Sirian Galactic Family. Of course, you have to do the inner work yourself, but you are greatly supported.

We cannot express what an honor it is to finally transmit this information to you after thousands and thousands of years. It took a while for the grass to grow, and we have patiently waited while holding you in our hearts. If and when you encounter darkness, remember the Sirian formula. Darkness has no power unless you give it your power. Darkness is merely a shadow that represents your blockages obscuring the One light. While it is easy to believe darkness is outside you, it never is, but you might see it embodied in others as a reminder to look within. Invalidating your shadow is like ignoring a vital organ. Just because you cannot see it does not mean it isn't there. And just because it plays out in dramas that seem to come from outside you, that does not mean it is not a reflection of you on some level. It is as much a part of you as a vital organ is to your body.

This lesson was a key to the awakening of my Galactic Family. Remember the Sirian formula. The first phase is to resist the temptation to push away the dark or the light; that is only a habit. When you sufficiently let go of all temptation to act habitually and you can sit on the razor's edge, the next step is to go deep into self-honesty. Find the parts of you that crave and the parts that fear. Sit with them. Know them. They are your friends, teachers, and eventually they are the keys to your freedom.

See with Neutral Eyes

The Sirian formula seems very philosophical. Could you give an example of how we can use it in our lives as human beings?

There are so many ways the formula can be used. We will give you a dramatic example. Let's say you are part of a spiritual group. The leader says, "I am going to give you a special training that is only for the chosen 144,000 people on your world who will awaken. To receive this teaching, you have to pledge your loyalty to me."

What starts to happen in the ego? It gets stimulated with thoughts of being special or gaining power. It wants to be recognized by the leader. These are cravings of the shadow. In addition, the ego might then start to feel fear and have thoughts of, "What do I have to give up to get this special gift?" or "I am afraid to go into the unknown." This is fear of the shadow.

How do you make the decision about whether or not to pledge your loyalty to the leader? It is not a mental process, but it seems so to humans. You think about it, but you will never get your answer that way. Instead, it requires you to go deep within and explore your cravings and fears as they relate to this issue. Really see yourself naked without judgment. Repeating this work, over and over, trains you to move to the point of paradox where you can see your cravings and fears with neutral eyes.

When you can see the situation with these neutral eyes, then the path ahead becomes crystal clear. You then move with the flow of the universe in a way that is not dictated by the polarized mind and emotions.

Hint: If you are ever asked to pledge your loyalty to someone instead of connecting to the universe directly, then you have acted from the craving or fear of the shadow.

Since you mentioned this idea of 144,000 people, is it really true? What is this all about?

It is meaningless, meaningless, meaningless. Do not go down that road. It was originally meant as a metaphor to describe the point of critical mass, but the number has no special meaning now. When you are presented with something that has the potential to grab your ego's attention, we suggest you step away. Hopefully, the example we provided shows you how the ego can get caught in its desire for specialness. We need to be blunt about this. We are not as polite as the Pleiadians.

There Is Always a Lesson

Years ago, I was studying under a very good channel, but she was very strict, saying that she would leave us behind if we struggled to keep up. Eventually, she gave up her work and stopped channeling. I experienced the emotion of abandonment by a teacher, which was very painful. Could you talk about that?

There is something to be learned from every teacher, even the most toxic and confused. There is always a lesson. The universe will always tell you when it is time to move on, and sometimes that message comes in painful ways. This particular lesson is an important one because humanity's biggest archetypal wound is abandonment. Your Galactic Family seemingly abandoned you long ago, and you have carried that wound like a painful scar for millennia.

You can work with this wound by using the Sirian formula. Let yourself feel the craving to fill the void left behind by the teacher. See and honor the craving to find a teacher who will never abandon you. That is phase one, the first level of freedom.

In phase two, let yourself be more conscious and discerning when choosing a teacher. Don't choose from the need to fill the abandonment wound. Don't choose the first teacher that comes along, because often the ego wants to fill the wound quickly by choosing a charismatic teacher with little substance. Resist that craving.

Do not make this a mental process, even though it seems that way. It is a different type of navigation that has more to do with clear self-observation. Slow down. Really see yourself. When the right choice comes, you will know it.

Remember, the right choice doesn't necessarily mean the pleasant one or the one in which you can gain the most knowledge. The right choice often means the right choice for what you need to learn, which you might not consciously understand at the time. That is why intuition is key. Your choices then become conscious instead of based on wounds.

We have one final idea to share: All teachers are human beings. Perhaps they are one step ahead of you in your growth in certain areas, but no matter what they say, they are also human. They don't have special powers; they have talents honed over many lives. Teachers are meant to be your friends and your guides. When you think of them in any way that emphasizes their specialness or their powers, you reinforce the idea of separation and empower the ego.

If a teacher ever says, "I am special. I am an expert. I am the only one with this information. You can only get it from me," then please run in the opposite direction. This egoic proclamation can also be communicated subtly in the energy of the teacher. That type of consciousness was rampant in the past 13,000 years and can no longer sustain itself. It often leads to a darker road. You are all free. Do not pick up the chains again.

The next 13,000 years will be about the community you will create with your galactic family as you walk the same road Home together. As with any journey, you must always take the first step.

THIRTEEN

The Road to Integration

SASHA

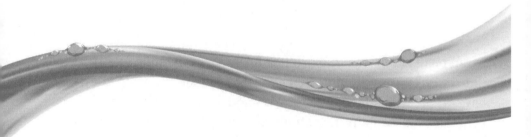

In what we have shared thus far, you understand the general idea of the small self being a fractal of the One holographic consciousness. These fractals, in various shapes and sizes, ripple out through time. You have experienced your incarnational journey in this fractalization through many different galactic species. Through the work we do together and your meditations and other types of journeys, you have interacted with some of your other fractals.

We share the following diagram to provide you with some symbolic structure that explains more unstructured and nonlinear information. This diagram provides insight into the two main galactic lineages — Lyran and Vegan — that have created an expression of polarity within your galactic family. Since we do not wish to go off on a tangent about galactic history, this is just an overview to show you the relationship between various civilizations.

The big blue circle represents the Lyran lineage. To review, the

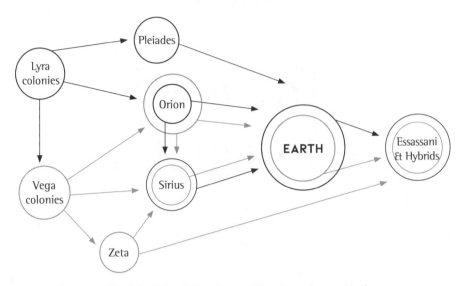

Figure 13.1. The Galactic Family Tree (Lyra and Vega lineage) created by Germane.

Lyran civilization was in existence for many millennia, and its evolutionary cycle was very long. Being the first humanoid group, they didn't have other civilizations to act as role models. The constellation you call Lyra does not contain the actual stars from that time, but they are in the same general direction. Lyran life spread far and wide, and Lyran colonies birthed many civilizations. We have mentioned the civilizations of Cassiopeia, Ursa Major (the Big Dipper), Ursa Minor (the Little Dipper), and Cygnus, which were all Lyran colonies in the ancient days. The ancient Lyran civilizations had to make their way through the realm of physicality and polarity just as you are doing now.

At some point, a group split off from the Lyran colonies and became another lineage, which is in gray on the map. This is the Vegan lineage. Again, the star Vega you see in the sky is not the original star system, but it marks the general direction. In linear measurement, the original system wasn't very far from your Sun.

As we have mentioned, civilizations in both the Lyran and Vegan lineages experienced the same three eras of evolution. The first era is the young species, when wounds begin emerging. The second era is healing, and the third era is integration and awakening. The two poles shaped how consciousness would experience polarity in your galactic family. This polarity would eventually move toward integration.

The Move toward Integration

Germane created the diagram, and he views it as a kind of map to show you how energy eventually moves toward complete integration through the galactic family. Let us explain further. Lyran energy split and became the Pleiadian civilization. The Vegan lineage had many offshoots, just like the Lyran lineage. It would be impossible to trace them all, so we only examine the major players in the galactic drama that most affect Earth. Next we move to Zeta, again in gray. You've already learned the generalities about the Zeta civilization.

As we progress on the map, you find that after the original separation and polarization into the two main lineages, the energy started to mix back together. Once polarity is expressed, there really is nowhere else to go but back to the One. Because your true nature is integration, you are always eventually drawn back to the Big Self. As we've said, one of the ways separation maintains in a physical reality is through the mechanism of the ego, which is like an anchor. Ego is a neutral idea and nothing negative. It is simply a mechanism — an anchor that keeps consciousness focused in the physical realm and in separation for a specific purpose. In third density, this metaphorical anchor is quite heavy, because you need a really strong mechanism to keep you separated from your natural state of One consciousness.

As you start moving into fourth density, as humanity is doing now, the idea of the ego as an anchor begins to change. It is still heavy enough to keep you in separation, but it gets lighter and does not interfere as much in the reintegration and awakening process. This is when you start experiencing dual levels of consciousness. You can only sustain polarized consciousness for a limited amount of time because your true nature is one of integration. The purpose of evolutionary cycles is to eventually bring poles together, leading to integration. This is a natural process. Consciousness doesn't have a timetable, so evolution moves slowly in galactic time.

Sometimes a civilization really struggles with integration to the point where, on the outside, it can look like the species is failing to integrate. This was the case in the early Orion civilization until their rapid awakening in the third era. During times when it seems like a civilization isn't evolving, consciousness sometimes migrates to other star systems in a fresh attempt at integration. But migrating consciousness always brings with it the seeds of polarity from its previous experience.

Looking at the Orion civilization on the map, you can see that it was genetically and culturally influenced by both the Lyran and Vegan lines. Lyran influence came in the form of their reverence for warriors and the focus on external reality. An authoritarian structure also came from Lyra, along with their incessant need for control and maintaining structure, which are very masculine traits.

The Vegan influence in Orion can be seen in high intellect. Orions connected with their emotional bodies, but they also funneled that energy through their minds. They were brilliant strategists. When they activated their warrior energy, they would often temporarily push down their emotional energy and channel it into war. The Orion civilization was similar to the Lyran and Vegan civilizations in that many star systems connected to the Orion lineage spread far and wide. The Orion civilization was the first attempt to integrate polarity through the Vegan and Lyran lines coming together. Eventually, some of the consciousness within Orion integrated itself and awakened, but it was a long road. Before that happened, the energy moved to other places to attempt integration. One of those places was Earth.

What happens when individual souls, or a group of souls in a civilization, aren't ready to let go of polarity? If they are still focused on the need to control and the majority of the collective energy is moving toward integration, they migrate some place else. Lines on the map connect Orion and Earth, because a good portion of that unintegrated energy from Orion came to Earth. Most third-density polarized civilizations are still in the middle of their integration process, so it is perfectly natural for there to be a migration of energy to an energetically compatible planet as a way to continue the galactic integration process.

This is why you see such a great degree of polarity on Earth. It permeates your entire society, and you can see it reflected in politics, religion, and the like. As you have just begun entering a fourth-density cycle, energy naturally accelerates. Accelerated energy always brings to the surface what you need to release or see. If a collective chooses not to release, see, or embrace the darker energies it has locked within, that energy has to move somewhere. With Orion, that energy moved to Earth. That is why the map shows gray and black circles for Orion: Energy came from two different lineages in an attempt to integrate.

Let us now look at the circles labeled Sirius. Lines of influence come from Vega, Zeta, and Orion. Compared to most members of your galactic family, the Sirians are a younger species. They are not just confined to the Sirius system but also associated with many stars in that general direction. The Sirian system also attempted massive integration. You can see that reflected in all the lines of influence coming from Vega, Zeta, Orion, and Lyra (through Orion). The Sirian system most influenced Earth, and they have been your mentors for millennia.

As with most civilizations, the Sirians had big challenges with their integration process in ancient days, as we discussed in previous chapters. They were often pulled in many directions. Looking at the Vegan influence within the Zetas, for example, the Zetas always defaulted to the mind. As the Sirians evolved, they saw this tendency in the Vegan line, and they tried to stop that tendency in themselves. The Sirians did a lot of work to integrate their mental and emotional bodies. They have a dark past that came from Orion influence, as you can see in figure 13.1. During one point in history, a split occurred between those who wished to evolve and integrate and those who clung to power and darker energies. The energy within Sirius not ready to integrate moved to your solar system — first to Mars and then to Earth.

Earth: a Final Stop on the Road to Integration

If you look at the diagram, it is shaped something like a sideways funnel. In the ancient days, consciousness spread throughout many systems. Now it's as if it is forced down a funnel of integration. Earth is one of the last significant stops in terms of integration. Overall, you don't have many other options to continue separation within your galactic family tree. The lineages that were once separated are coming back together.

Earth is influenced by many different energies, as you can see in the diagram. The pattern of Earth's evolution will likely be very similar to the paths of Sirius and Orion, because the three of you have a very strong triad of energy. Your civilizations contain multiple threads of influence, and you are doing the work to facilitate integration on a very deep level. Earth has the same choice as its Galactic Family: You will either integrate and awaken or kick the can down the road to another future potential civilization that will carry the remnants of your unfinished business.

As we view the probability lines now, we do not see any other place being created to channel unfinished energy. That means it is will be integrated here. That is a tremendous amount of pressure. You feel this pressure individually and as a mass conscious. If you engage this pressure, it accelerates your evolution. If you resist the pressure, it turns inward. When it turns inward, it can create inner pain, mental illness, and physical disease.

Humanity has a choice. How will you respond to this pressure to integrate? The pressure isn't coming from outside you. It has to do with your natural state of consciousness, which is already integration. Since you've passed the point of deepest separation, it is like a snowball rolling down a hill. It builds speed and mass as it careens down the hill. That is why you feel such pressure now.

Let us move to the final circles labeled "Essassani & Hybrids." To simplify, Essassani (the Sassani people) represent one of the hybrid species created from Zetas and humans. Integration happens on many levels, all the way from consciousness to the physical levels of DNA. If and when beings come together, integration also happens on the species level. The Essassani system and other hybrid species represent the next stop on this road of integration. The hybrids contain all the threads of the tapestry that originated in Lyra. It is the point of coming Home. When a planet begins working with Hybrids, as you have begun to do, it means you are approaching the potential of this integration point. This is why Hybrid-7 showed himself in the photo [figure 12.1, chapter 12], to remind you of the road ahead.

Hybrids have accelerated their contact on Earth. Earth has Lyran and Vegan influence, and Sirius has Vegan influence. So Hybrid-7 and most hybrids are an integrative nexus point. As you interact with hybrid energy, it is like connecting to the Omega point — the end point of the integration process. Those of you doing this kind of work are pioneers, clearing the path with a machete, so to speak, helping to create the road through which humanity and future civilizations will travel.

May we also remind you that the hybrids are your future selves. Because of this, contact with them is significant to your consciousness fractal. If you are at the point where you have integrated your shadow and you are open enough to allow hybrid energy into your consciousness and recognize it as an aspect of you, then you are integrating your whole galactic history. Hybrid-7's appearance, and contact with other hybrids, is like a barometer of your evolutionary process.

Twenty to thirty short years ago, humans had a lot of fear about Zetas, hybrids, and abduction. Much of this was because the inner shadow was still not widely recognized as a valid part of you that needed processing and honoring. You often projected your fears onto the outer world as a way to force the integration process. (No one was doing this to you. It is just the way denied energy moves.) The saga of the abduction phenomenon and the primal fear it generated allowed humanity to process its collective fear and begin the shadow work without even knowing it. This was an important time, and for the most part, while there are still those who subscribe to negative ET stories, your collective has released its attachment to the fear scenarios enough to move to the next step in your evolution. Those negative stories are distortions, and they distract you from doing necessary inner work. This evolutionary process is a frightening one, but it is a necessary step on the road to integration.

We know some people are still stuck in the drama of fearful scenarios. But more than ever before, you are starting to see that kind of habitual fear is a reflection of older, inner, unhealed wounds. There is no reason to judge those souls still stuck there, but know they will stay stuck until they look at the wound within that reinforces a belief in conspiratorial and negative dramas. They will always see a bogeyman. The bogeymen have been the Zetas for decades now, but even that is changing. The archetypal bogeyman is only useful to help you see your shadow.

The Nature of the Universe Is to Grow

Returning to the idea of kicking the can down the road, do the Essassani and other hybrids exist as a solution to a problem only if we don't heal the wounds here? Is their existence contingent on us not evolving, or are they going to exist anyway?

Everything happens simultaneously. They exist anyway. We

previously talked about the Orion system. When they went through their transformation, a huge wave of ascension happened, but some souls didn't finish the healing process. The Essassani and hybrids are playing the role of a receptacle, if you will, for consciousness ready to move into a higher integrated state. That role is always needed. That's why we said they are your future selves.

If you are referring to a culmination, does that mean an end? It just doesn't seem like there can be an end, so there must be more beyond that.

The idea of a beginning and an end is linear. A more accurate way to look at it is to compare it to the cycles of nature with the seasons, for example. As above, so below. These cycles of nature also reflect the cycles of consciousness movement. In-breath and out-breath, winter and summer, male and female — these are all expressions of existence when you move away from the center point. What do we mean by that? Let us return to the infinity symbol.

Figure 13.2. The dot on the center of the infinity symbol represents the One consciousness at rest.

If you draw a dot at the exact center point of the infinity symbol, it represents the One consciousness that you are. This is the point of the One hologram of everything that exists. It is at rest. When the One consciousness is completely at rest, it might be a lovely place to exist, but the nature of the universe is to grow. With the cycles of consciousness we previously mentioned, you can see that it eventually needs to expand. When consciousness goes into a cycle of growth, it needs an energy source.

The best analogy for that energy source is a battery. It has a positive charge and a negative charge, and your device cannot operate without that dynamic. These positive and negative charges are not good or bad; they simply represent opposite charges. As consciousness leaves its rest state, it moves into duality. That duality creates the energy charge that facilitates growth and evolution.

The One taps into this energy source as a way to fuel its exploration and expansion. We recognize that we have to speak linearly for these cycles to be understood, but this process happens simultaneously.

The human mind can only witness it linearly. Thus, you can say that this dualistic cycle represents the out-breath (creation) and the in-breath (integration). You on Earth are now experiencing the aspect of the cycle that corresponds to the in-breath. These cycles are very long, but from the cosmic point of view, they happen in a moment. The in-breath and out-breath occur in one cosmic moment. That is the paradox.

When the majority of consciousness on Earth is ready to advance, what will happen to those who are not ready? Where will they go?

Please consider that the galactic lineage diagram is a fluid idea. The time continuum is not an issue. For those not ready to integrate, they can choose to move to first-era or second-era Orion or Sirius, or somewhere else still processing polarity. There are myriad choices where you can still experience separation and polarity. The One consciousness is a hologram in which every time continuum and every conceivable possibility is a fractal. Your consciousness will move to the fractal that resonates with whatever is left unhealed.

It isn't as if another planet has to be created to help you process polarity, but that can happen. You can just move to another realm within the fractal still processing what you need to process. Again, we speak linearly, but it isn't a linear process.

If that is the case, then why did Orion awaken? Why did we come to Earth instead of going back to a previous time in Orion to heal ourselves?

The combination of energies in Orion is not quite the same as the combination of energies on Earth. The influences on Earth are actually more integrated than they were in Orion, because they are a result of much processing over millennia. The energy is more refined.

The 13,000-Year Cycle of Integration

Does the 26,000-year cycle discussed by the Maya connect to all this?

Yes. To put it as simply as possible, the evolutionary energy of your galaxy moves according to the principles of a torus field, which you can see in the diagram below. We've drawn a line to represent the "arm" of your galaxy. Your Sun is on the outer part of the arm, and it takes approximately 26,000 years for your Sun to make a complete cycle relative to the Central Sun — the center of your galaxy. This

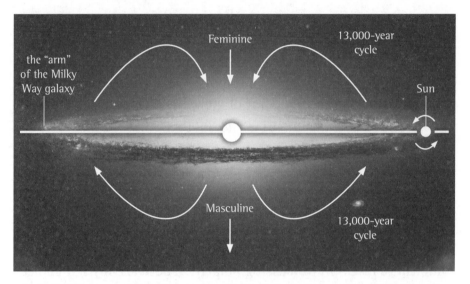

Figure 13.3. The energy of humans moving from third to fourth density through the 26,000-year cycle.

means there are two 13,000-year cycles. One cycle is when your Sun's position is below the line, and the other cycle is when it is above the line. There are two important things to remember about this cycle. The first is that the bottom part of the cycle, where the arrows emerge from the torus field, is a projective/masculine part of the cycle. This is the period when civilizations generally go to sleep and experience their most separated, third-density cycle. In your time, that is approximately 13,000 years. We have called this your Atlantean cycle, and you recently finished it around 2012.

The top part of the cycle, where the arrows show energy moving into the torus, is the integrative/feminine part of the cycle. This usually marks when a civilization moves into a fourth-density cycle. It starts to awaken and heal. We call this your Lemurian cycle. You have recently entered this part of the cycle and are still in a transitional phase from one to the other. These transitional phases are intense and mark times of profound change.

Your Earth has had the opportunity to awaken and fully integrate many times, which is common for most planets. You had this opportunity during the Lemurian era on your world, approximately 13,000 to 26,000 years ago, but it was not yet time. You fell into sleep again for another 13,000 years. All this has to do with the supportive energy of the galactic torus field. When a planet is in its masculine/projective phase, the strongest energy is separation. When a planet is in its feminine/integrative phase, it gets pulled along in the tide of integration and, if ready, it eventually awakens.

We know humans can become depressed thinking these cycles just repeat over and over again. That is not so. Evolution is not a circle, but a spiral. Each complete cycle leads you to another, more refined cycle until you reach the implosion point — integration.

You are now propelled by galactic energy toward integration. This is what we meant by "feeling the pressure" — the unstoppable galactic evolutionary cycle. You have the opportunity to integrate and ascend as a planet within this coming cycle. If you don't, there will be other opportunities. There are always myriad opportunities, as we have mentioned, either here or in another place and time.

Remember, you are all fractals of the One. The evolutionary process is actually not singular, even though you have seemingly singular experiences. In truth, your singular selves aren't going "here" and "there" on the map. That is only a useful illusion that assists you with evolution.

As you begin to resonate more with your collective and integrated nature, you will see and feel the evolutionary process on a collective level in a more visceral way. You truly exist on every level in every time. Therefore, in the end, it really doesn't matter where you do your evolutionary work. You will be energetically attracted to the resonance you need for the next phase of your evolution.

FOURTEEN

The Sirian Evolutionary Journey

SASHA AND HAMÓN

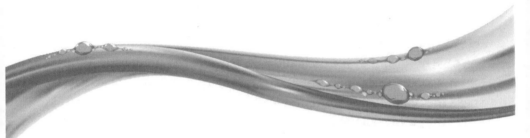

Sasha: When discussing the galactic lineage map, we implied it is complete. By this, we mean no missing pieces need to be integrated. There are now many places on the map where integration can happen. Thus, it is a matter of choice and resonance where on the map your soul wants to go to integrate whatever it needs.

A few years ago, the Sirian ambassador Hamón began to channel some very profound information for you. Now, he also brings specific energy. We have talked about how Sirian consciousness is really the closest to human consciousness, both in terms of lineage and character. For this reason, Sirians can serve as powerful models for humanity as you move forward on your integrative journey. Much energetic exchange takes place between humans and Sirians, as it has for thousands of years.

We have also talked about the ancient schools given by ETs, primarily Sirian and Pleiadian, during Earth's infancy. The Galactic

Family began to plant seeds to nestle inside human consciousness as you experienced growth through the galactic cycles. As you grew, these seeds sprouted. We have joked about how patient the Sirians are, that they don't mind watching the grass grow. Their understanding of time is always from the big picture, so they don't mind long evolutionary journeys. This patience and nurturing is natural for them, and they enjoy engaging the process. They are infinitely patient in waiting for the correct time to fertilize the seeds and then support the blossoming.

The ancient humans who were the first recipients of the teachings from the School of the Nine Serpents eventually became the original priests and priestesses. Many of them were human-Sirian or human-Pleiadian hybrids, which meant their lives spanned about 800 to 1,000 years. This longevity was important for the teachings to be consistent and focused as they were passed down to future generations in an efficient and continuous way.

As we mentioned, your Galactic Family left the planet for a time. Then it was the responsibility of these hybrid priests and priestesses to pass the teachings to humans. As time went by and the ETs did not return, the gene pool began to dilute. Their life spans shortened. With shorter life spans and the sense of loss that came from the departure of their ET mentors, the continuity of the teachings became more difficult to maintain. As the planet entered a 13,000-year cycle of masculine energy and disintegration, it became difficult to maintain and remember the true essence of the teachings. Sometimes they were misunderstood and turned into religions.

The seeds went back into the soil, so to speak, and became temporarily dormant. Once the 13,000-year cycle of disintegration ended, it was as if the soil was watered again and the seeds could sprout.

Here you are in a new cycle of integration. The seeds are sprouting again, and new opportunities await humanity. The energy that originally helped plant the seeds has returned to support you once more. After 2012, beings such as Hamón renewed their work. As we did in the ancient days, we have joined his efforts, which is why the School of the Nine Serpents has reemerged. It is also one reason why this information is often delivered at venues in or near natural environments. The Sirians are very focused on the idea of sensation —

the wind, sun, air, or anything that brings your full presence into integration in the physical realm. He will now talk about why this is important.

Teachings of Sensation

Hamón: Hello, my friends. Let us talk once again about ancient Sirian history. As you have seen, we were influenced by both the Vegan and Lyran lineages. You have also seen from the diagram that we were influenced by Orion as well. During a period in my people's history, we had a bit of an identity crisis. We had so much influence from our Galactic Family that we didn't understand our own story. But we were clear about one thing: We knew we could not follow the road of the Vegans and Zetas. We knew we could not cut off our hearts and emotions from our experiences. Even knowing this, our genetic tendency to invalidate emotions was quite strong.

We did much inner work to maintain our connections to the emotional body instead of moving our awareness solely into the mental body. We call this process of remaining fully emotionally present "full incarnation." Many species incarnate but hold themselves back from full incarnation because of how painful it is. Many species resist full incarnation as a way to protect themselves from pain. But the paradox is that you must fully incarnate in order to return Home. This is why we created the School of the Nine Serpents in the ancient days. It became a road map to help humans fully incarnate and experience separation in the way it is meant to be experienced. Why fragment from the Source in order to have the experience of separation and then not let yourself fully experience it? That only prolongs suffering and the evolutionary process.

Through the School of the Nine Serpents teachings, we created tools to assist you in fully incarnating. One of these tools has to do with sensation. What do we mean by that? It is impossible to fully incarnate if your mind is "over there," your emotions are somewhere else, and you ignore the sensory data from your physical body. You become fragmented. This fragmentation stops you from becoming whole and experiencing life as an integrated being. We created opportunities for students to harness the energies of sensation for their own awakening process. You can feel sensations externally through the physical body and internally through the emotional or mental body. You must learn to use all sensations — internal and external — to fuel the awakening process. As soon as you push away the undesirable, the disintegration process begins.

You can see, then, that our character is to never run away. We learned to never run away from what we didn't want to experience. We taught ourselves to experience everything without judgment, which is a difficult thing to learn. This might seem hardcore to humans, but to us, the amount of energy it takes to constantly push things away is much more hardcore. This process is not for the faint of heart, however. In the ancient days, many from my species would not go into their pain. Those who refused to do this inner work began to split off energetically. As they went further into denial and separation, they began to pull in the darker influences from the Orion lineage.

Returning to the idea of integration, we can liken the process to a snowball rolling down a hill. Sasha has talked about the galactic lineage map as a complete system. As with a snowball, you feel the most momentum the closer it gets to the bottom of the hill. The snowball gets very heavy and is harder to stop. Just like you are experiencing now, my ancient people felt this great momentum toward integration. Most followed that flow. Those who resisted had the capacity to harness and redirect great amounts of energy to temporarily fuel their separation. That was when the Sirian dark secret societies began.

That momentum toward integration, harnessed in a twisted way by those who refused to integrate, became the energy that supported the dark groups that began to form. These groups did not like the feeling of losing control, as when a snowball rolls down a hill. They wanted to be in control at all times. This was why they pulled in first-era and second-era Orion energy, as a way to keep working on the issue of control. To use an analogy, we can compare the dark Orion energy to lemonade. Dark Sirian energy was more like lemon juice concentrate. It was extremely focused and intense. Looking at this from a bigger picture, it was a way to further refine the polarized energy of the entire galactic family.

As you can see, my people were deeply divided in the ancient days. It created much tension within our civilization. To give you a reference point on parallel time tracks, these negative Sirian groups were active on your Earth during the Atlantean era. Later civilizations included ancient Babylonia, Sumeria, and Egypt. Ancient Egypt pulled in a lot of energy from these old dark schools. That was when black magic schools on your Earth began to form.

Collective Shame

There are two significant things to remember. The first is that while dark energy seems overwhelming, it represented only a small percentage of Sirian influence on your planet in the ancient days. The negative side usually appears to have the loudest voice. Secondly, in the early part of the last 13,000-year cycle, you were influenced by two Sirian groups — positive mentors and dark-arts practitioners. This is one reason your mythology seems so polarized and filled with heroes and villains. Most reflect this intense energy that played out on Earth as you entered your recent sleep cycle that is now ending.

If you look at the galactic-lineage map, you see a large influence from Sirians on Earth. The influence was both positive and negative. You bring in so much of this energy, much like a blender making a smoothie. You are a kind of integration factory for all this energy, for Earth and the entire galactic family. As previously discussed, my ancient people felt a lot of shame for this influence on Earth. Reincarnationally, many of you had lives in this ancient Sirian time. Because of this, humanity now holds the residual shame left unhealed in its collective unconscious.

Some of these Sirian past lives contained experiences of being a victim or a perpetrator of the dark arts. Some of you were unwitting perpetrators, which created even more shame. As you now hurl yourself toward integration, all this hidden shame is revealed. You have a limited time to hide wounds in the unconscious before they come to the surface.

Many of you who do deep inner work feel shame, and you don't know why. Some of it could be individual wounds, but some is on the collective level from the migration of Sirian energy. On Earth, as you accelerate your integration, this wound of shame carried by your Sirian Galactic Family (your past selves) begins to reveal itself. This shame is in the hologram of creation you are a part of, so it can never be denied. Please know this is already beginning to heal.

One of the games polarized consciousness likes to play is creating stories. We've mentioned that polarized consciousness makes up stories about negative ETs, cover-ups, and conspiratorial dramas. Consciousness only knows how to process the energy from that polarized state. But this totally removes you from the truth of the integration process. The more you spin stories of conspiracies and victimization by ETs and other bogeymen, the more you keep yourself from riding the wave of integration. Instead, you keep yourself in disintegration and chaos. This is one of the reasons why many channeled teachers do not talk about conspiracy stories; it triggers too much polarization and distraction and only empowers disintegration.

We have said it before: There is no bogeyman outside you. There are only fractal reflections of you in every probability that exists. The tidal wave of integration is happening, my dears, and you have the choice to ride the wave or resist it. The undertow of resistance is very painful. We recommend surfing the wave.

The Sirius System
Regarding Sirius A and Sirius B, is there anything you wish to share about that binary star system?

Please understand that humans delineated the Sirian system that way. Our view of star systems is very different from yours. We consider your Sun to be Sirius C. This is how intricately entwined you are with your Sirian heritage. In the ancient days, well before Sumeria, regular circuits of ETs came through the Sirian system that included your Sun.

Many people ask us about the Annunaki, thinking they were a specific species. The Annunaki, in ancient Earth languages, means something similar to, "Those who came from the sky, the children of Anu." (Anu was a well-known ancient ET figure.) Annunaki referred to ETs in general and not a specific race; they contained multiple races.

In those ancient days, large planet-ships housing many beings traveled slowly between star systems. Regular circuits of travel took ships through the Sirian system and the local star neighborhood, including your Sun. This is where the myths of the Nibiru come from. Whenever one of these planet-ships arrived, humanity was influenced in some way, in science, art, or philosophy. These circuits were predictable in the ancient days, so people on Earth always knew when the next planet-ship was coming.

Please remember that visitations to your solar system are ancient. We have already spoken about Mars, which had a thriving civilization well before the Atlantean era on your planet. Mars was the first place in your solar system that attempted the integration process you are now experiencing on Earth.

Here is a version of your galactic-lineage map including Mars. All the same influences — Lyra, Vega, Sirius, and Orion — are true for Mars as they are for Earth.

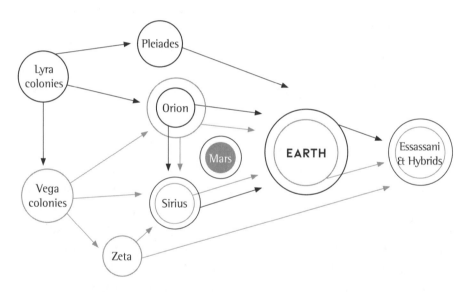

Figure 14.1. Mars shown in its position on the Galactic Family Tree.

Some dark groups were on Mars, including dark Sirian schools. All of this added to the conflicts prevalent at that time in your solar system. The original intention was for Mars to be a home for the Association of Worlds — a kind of UN for the galactic family. But attempts to create integrated structures during disintegrative times could not withstand those polarized energies.

Now that you have entered a new cycle, some of you are beginning to connect with ancient Martian beings. Even though they might refer to themselves as Martian, they come from the Vegan lineage.

After all, the Vegan star system wasn't far from yours in the ancient days. Mars was influenced by some of the old authoritarian Lyrans, but most of its heritage was Vegan.

When we speak of the migration of dark energies from Sirius, Mars was like a stopover point for that migration, and dark magicians were certainly present on ancient Mars. In a sense, it was like a microcosm of unhealed Orion energy. As you read in chapter 11, this is one reason it was important for the Mars Guardian to seal the planet's energy until Earth moved into its integrative cycle. Now that you have moved into the integrative galactic cycle, Martian energy can reemerge without triggering too much pain. This integrative cycle also weakens the temptation to return to darkness for those of you still processing dark energy from the ancient past.

We do not wish to talk any more about this dark energy. We know humans are curious, but we still feel it is something best left in the past. For now, we wish to share with you a powerful meditation exercise after a brief explanation of its significance.

✻ EXERCISE ✻
Sirian Pineal Gland Exercise

We have spoken about the School of the Nine Serpents and how ancient Sirians and Pleiadians trained humans through these schools all over the world. The spirit of the teachings was the same, but the styles differed. The Pleiadian style was more feminine and heart-centered, such as the teachings of the Golden Lake. The Sirian style was a bit more masculine, using the pineal gland. It included a lot of consciousness science that came from the Vegan heritage, such as the Sirian formula.

We wish to share some pineal work with you that is classically Sirian. This kind of work can help those of you who get pineal headaches when energy increases. Please begin by getting yourself comfortable. If you wish, read this meditation aloud while recording it to play each time you practice.

- As you relax, rest your attention somewhere in the center of your brain; the location does not have to be exact.
- Go deep within your brain and sense a particular spot where consciousness can rest. This is the interface from cosmic

consciousness into human reality — a black hole and white hole in the center of the brain.

- As you rest your consciousness there, cones of energy expand from that center point and extend in all directions. Don't worry if you cannot see them. These cones are like antennae or receiving dishes for cosmic energy in all directions.
- On the inhale, breathe cosmic energy in from the cosmos through all the cones to the center of your brain.
- On the exhale, release energy through all the cones out into the cosmos. This represents the cosmic exchange from Oneness (in-breath) to separation (out-breath).
- Repeat this cycle as you continue your breaths.

We recommend that you practice this exercise often. In the weeks, months, and years ahead, it will facilitate the expansion of your consciousness. Now we will walk you through a more accelerated version to give you a taste of this Sirian work. Rest here until you are ready to move ahead.

- Return your focus to the expansion of the cones as you receive cosmic energy; bring the energy deep into the center of your brain.
- As you do this, your awareness begins to take on a spherical shape. It grows and expands so that you clearly feel your body inside your spherical awareness. Your awareness is infinitely larger than your body. Your body nestles inside. Take a moment to explore this experience.
- Because your body is within your consciousness, your consciousness can feel every sensation the body feels. It does so from a detached state. If the wind brushes across your face (or whatever sensation is there), you feel it purely — without story, meaning, or reason. You simply feel pure sensation. Let yourself feel the wind. Nothing else exists. Your awareness is rooted in sensation.
- Shift to sound. You might hear many simultaneous sounds, such as traffic noise or buzzing insects. Feel the sensation of the sounds without thoughts interfering with the full experience. There is no story or commentary. There is just your absorption in the present sound in a hyper-present way.

- Now move your attention to your butt on the chair. Really feel the pressure of your flesh on the chair without thought, story, or commentary. Just feel it fully with no internal chatter.

Doing this exercise, your cones expand deeper into infinity. Your consciousness expands from focusing tightly on sensation. This practice comes from second-era Sirian history, when we began our awakening process. Remain in this open state as long as you wish. When you are ready, you may continue.

- Return now to the awareness of the cones stretching into infinity.
- Return to the center point of your brain.
- Become aware of your physical body so that consciousness now begins to reassemble into this physical reality.
- Your perception narrows and focuses on your body in this realm. Does your body need to move? If so, allow it to move or stretch.

This exercise has many aspects. One of them is to help you begin to allow two different states of consciousness to exist simultaneously — the hologram and the fractal. Experiencing this dual consciousness is absolutely essential for the next phase of your evolution on Earth.

FIFTEEN

Human Fractals and the Golden Lake

SASHA

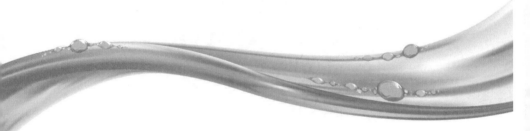

We have mentioned the idea of the consciousness hologram throughout this book, because it is one of the most
important recognitions humans can have about their true
nature. The recognition of this truth alone can dramatically shift the
trajectory of your planet. We want to return to the Pleiadian teachings of the Golden Lake, which are some of the feminine teachings of
the School of the Nine Serpents. The Golden Lake teachings explore
in depth the ideas of the hologram and the fractal as they relate to
consciousness.

We have found that one of the most valuable ways to express an
idea is through contrast. We have given this metaphor before, but we
offer it again to aid in your deeper understanding of what is and is not
holographic consciousness.

Let's say that I have a photo of an apple. I tear this photo into tiny
pieces. If you want to see the image of the complete apple in your

reality, you have to assemble the image of the apple from the tiny pieces, much like a jigsaw puzzle. This is how humans view reality in a third-density realm. Nothing is connected, and it seems as if people and experiences exist independent of each other.

Now let's imagine a different scenario. I tear the photo of the apple into tiny pieces again. This time, each tiny piece of the original photo contains the complete image of the apple. It doesn't matter how small I tear these pieces; the complete image of the apple remains. This represents holographic consciousness. Each small piece of the whole image is a fractal of the hologram. It is complete unto itself. It reflects the complete image, no matter the size. Figure 15.1 is a sample of fractal art.

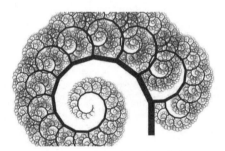

Figure 15.1. Fractal art of a spiral.

Let us bring this metaphor to your consciousness. If you look at the diverse array of individual beings on your world, you can see that you each have your own story and history. On the surface, it looks as if you are all separate. Coming together is like fitting yourselves together like a jigsaw puzzle, forcing people to have tolerance for each other, and so on. This is an old-fashioned understanding of collective consciousness that is not very accurate. Let us return to a familiar diagram [figure 15.2].

As a reminder, the outside circle represents the One consciousness (the hologram), and the inside circle represents the fragmentation experienced through incarnation (the fractal). This diagram is very simplistic, but it can aid your comprehension.

We are saying you are all fractals. You might temporarily turn away from each other as a way to have an individual experience. Even if you bump into each other or notice each other through your human

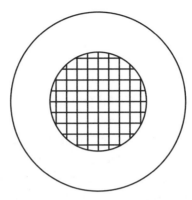

Figure 15.2. The representation of the transition from Oneness to separation (first shared in chapter 5).

relationships, it is unlikely that you recognize the other fractal as a reflection of you unless you have been doing this kind of work on a spiritual path. Humans generally don't recognize the complete image of the whole in another person, mostly because they don't recognize it within themselves.

Biblically, this is what you call "the fall." It was an experience of such deep separation that you turned away from the remembrance of your true nature. It isn't a punishment. You weren't kicked out of a garden. It is simply part of the evolutionary journey of third density. In this journey, you look at others and don't remember who you are. Actually, the opposite happens: You look at others and identify them as "other."

As you begin to move toward a fourth-density expression, the natural wave of evolutionary energy moves you away from that intense separation. You have little flashes of your wholeness. Those flashes are ephemeral at first, and you feel you can't grasp them. Those flashes get more frequent and happen for longer periods of time. When that happens, you begin noticing synchronicity in a way that causes you to sense the connectivity between yourself and others.

At this current phase of evolution on Earth, most of you have begun to feel that connectivity, but the mind still tells you the other person is separate. When you encounter someone whose beliefs or attitudes don't resonate with yours, you do not generally look within to see the part of you they trigger and know the other person is a mirror. This creates conflict, because your heart feels the connection, but your mind pushes it away. This is a very significant part of evolution, because the whole purpose of physicality is to get to a point of forgetfulness in order to savor the experience of awakening to your true nature again.

Part of the distress many of you feel has to do with this dichotomy. Your desire to open and connect combines with your habitual need to protect yourself. This is the irony of opening yourself to the universe. The opening process is not a doing, and that is part of the challenge. Humans cannot respond to a command to let go, but the spiritual ego often keeps demanding you do just that. It doesn't work that way. Letting go is a gradual process of relaxation within you. You can even say that letting go is "not doing." But the ego gets frustrated and thinks, "How do I not do?"

As your helpers and mentors, all we can do is plant the seeds of the idea of not doing and let those seeds grow until you start to understand what it feels like. You will learn that you cannot do the not doing.

The Community Hologram

We wish to share an idea that has puzzled humanity for a very long time. But first, let's look at fractal dynamics within group consciousness. Many on your world are interested in the idea of intentional communities. For example, you have ten people who come together because, on the surface, they have a common goal and belief system. This group gets a big farmhouse together and starts to build an intentional community. Time goes by, and what happens? Usually the group begins to disintegrate.

The same thing happens with spiritual organizations. Perhaps people who follow a guru come together with an idea of peace and love. Later, it is as if the rot in the group rises to the surface with drama, competition, and challenge. The group either falls apart or holds itself together through the illusion of a perfect community. And let us not forget your Lyran Galactic Family and the forced utopias of the Cygnus civilization. Why does this happen?

Let's examine the fractal metaphor with a story: You have a torn photo of an apple with the image of the apple fully present in each separated piece. Each fractal, or photo, of the full apple represents a person's consciousness. So let's say one fractal represents Bobbie's consciousness. Her fractal contains everything: love, pain, shame, and a shadow, because everyone has a shadow. But Bobbie's shadow is deeply buried. All members of the community have pieces of unprocessed energy within their fractal consciousness. Bobbie joins the community along with Harry and Ron. Let's say Ron really bugs Bobbie, and her anger is triggered when Ron unintentionally pushes Bobbie's buttons. What is going on? When you have a community that does not fully understand and embrace the knowledge that they are all fractals of each other, then the fault for disharmony always projects outward to another person. No one ever looks inward.

Continuing with the story, the community begins to dissolve. They become a community of five instead of ten. The five left are more compatible, and they live together for a while. Then Ben becomes very bothered by Harry, and the whole dynamic begins again. The community divides and boils down to the most compatible people left — the married couple Harry and Bobbie. They are the only two left. As time goes on, even Bobbie has had enough, and only Harry remains.

Harry sits by himself and feels the dichotomy. He feels the relief of being free of the community, but he also feels lonely. In his loneliness, he meditates. In his meditations, he sees the fractal of his own consciousness as being one with the hologram. Intuitively, he moves inward and creates a community of all his unhealed parts. He gathers all the parts of himself he has denied, hated, and shunned, and he begins to befriend them and let them be his teachers. He finds the darkest shadow within him, and he has a revelation. He sees that Bobbie, Ron, Ben, and all the others express the same fractal of consciousness. Perhaps they vary on the surface, but they are really one and the same. Through this revelation, Harry recognizes that when he looks at Bobbie or Ben, he actually sees himself. This is not a mental realization; it is a deeply profound awareness.

When people have these realizations, the entire consciousness of a planet changes. You might think Earth isn't at this evolutionary place yet, but many of you are making this realization, and the energy has started to change. You see that intentional communities don't work when people use them to escape the inner fractal and reject the reflective nature of the universe. You are indeed slowly realizing that you all contain the same fractal of the apple within you and that One consciousness stares through a multitude of eyes. You are beginning to realize the connection between all.

As you make this shift on an individual level, it spreads to the collective. When that happens, what do you see? You see huge resistance. Those of you caught in the fractal of separation and don't want to lose control or let go of your view of reality begin to resist. You create chaos and distraction to stop those around you from moving into the natural flow of evolution. You might sound the alarm about a "one world order" or any institution that, to you, means you must surrender your individuality and freedom, which are the main concerns of an insecure ego.

As we have said before, your natural state is as the One hologram, so the idea of stopping the process of healing and reintegration is an illusion. The tide cannot be stopped; it can only be delayed. Timing is the key. It is not yet time for all the pieces to come together, because much healing still needs to be done. When you are truly healed, the collective will have no more fear about the integration of consciousness and thus no more need to create fearful stories to try to stop the process.

A student of past workshops sent Lyssa the following question. We include it here because it is very applicable to what we've been talking about and what so many of you now experience.

I have been feeling less and less interested in spiritual matters. I'm a little disgusted with where mystery-school teachings and the "manifestation movement" is going. The idea of awakening has been hijacked by people pushing conspiracy theories, and the interest in psychedelics makes it all sound like a shallow party. I feel exhausted in life, and I just want to sleep or be at home with my dogs and my family. I just want a normal job — not a healing job or a spiritual job. It feels very strange.

While this woman might not realize the place she has gotten to in her consciousness, this is what happens when you have a dawning realization that nothing "out there" is going to make you happier, accelerate your growth, or expand your awareness. This realization begins deep within your consciousness, and you slowly recognize the illusory nature of reality. When this happens, a type of death process begins in the ego structure. This is a very good thing, actually, but it feels uncomfortable. Such a realization brings emotional pain, anger, and apathy. This is the beginning of the death process of the more superficial aspects of your ego. You can consider this a good sign. It can initiate a very deep integration process if you are willing to do your inner work.

Transformation of the Ego

This brings up the issue of the ego. We've talked about this in so many different ways, but we have to say, once again, that the ego isn't a negative thing. It is purely a mechanism to help you organize and experience a separated reality. In my Pleiadian reality, my people are still physical, but we have had a longer time to evolve than humans. We have been able to observe the shift that happens in the ego during the transition from third to fourth density. In deepest third density, the ego is the strongest, and fractals do not want to see reflections of themselves. You've gone through that deepest separation already, and now you might feel the third-density version of your ego-suit is too small for you — like a wetsuit squeezing you. To transform the ego to a fourth-density version, you have to cut holes or disintegrate the ego-suit so that your true nature can breathe.

This "ego squeezing" is one reason people feel so much pain right now on individual and collective levels. Especially for those of you who have not been exploring spirituality, you might feel exhausted, as if you are treading water with your heads barely above the surface. You might not understand why you feel anxiety and depression. It is because the ego-suit of separation is beginning to feel like it is strangling you.

If you are reading this, then you have already begun to shed some of the pieces of the ego-suit that are constricting you. Recognizing your fractal nature in relationship to other fractals as well as the whole is part of the awakening process. While we assure you that all of this is normal, we know it is hard for you to trust the process. We have seen this process in the transitions of countless civilizations in your galactic family. While this squeezing is a product of accelerated energies, your expanding consciousness and outgrowing your ego-suit serves another important function: The pain and discomfort of this process can propel you to the next level if you allow it. Human nature is such that you often don't seek change until you are in pain. It does get better, my dear ones.

Let us go back to the fictional story of the community, especially

Harry as the community of one. Once the community dissolved, only Harry remained. What did he do? Because he was alone, all he could do was go inward and explore his own fractal. He looked into those dark corners where he previously never wanted to look. Through that inner work, he was able to transcend the projective nature of his third-density ego. He realized that he was projecting his own unhealed energy onto other people. He began to move himself more deeply into his fractal, seeing the reflective nature of the universe. As he began to shift in this way, he experienced a death/transition of the third-density ego, and his fourth-density ego mechanism — which is much less polarized — began to awaken. He began to embrace all other fractals that had seemed separate as a reflection of himself. In doing so, he began to awaken his holographic consciousness.

This might sound esoteric and unreachable, but it is happening now. This is how consciousness expands. Right now you have the gift of dual awareness. You are the fractal squeezed into your constrictive, skintight ego-suit. You are also experiencing the holographic self. Up until now, you have shoved your holographic self under the bed, so to speak. It was only allowed to peek out every now and then. It is now emerging more and more, bringing with it an exhilarating and terrifying feeling of vulnerability and openness.

This is a very tenuous stage of evolution for all civilizations. You might not agree, but we see that you are doing very well. The biggest work right now has to do with learning not to be distracted by the external world. If something triggers you in the external world, look within, even if it is something horribly dark. If it triggers you, then something deep within you seeks the light. You don't even have to understand what it is. You don't have to find out the details of a past life and work through it linearly as you did in the past, but that might happen organically. Because your holographic nature is coming online, you are working on levels that go beyond the linear understanding of your stories.

You have heard about the dark Sirian past and their shame. That is coming up as a gift to you now to give you the courage to heal your darkness. Many of you know the story of my Pleiadian heritage. When my people were very young as a species, they absolutely refused to see their inner shadows. Because they never processed anything negative, all that energy went into a metaphorical closet. As you know, closets have limited size; if you keep stuffing things in there, at some point the door will no longer close.

The tipping point for my species was when we had pushed down so much of our shadow that plagues began to emerge on our world. No one could cure them. On the medical level, no one could understand what was happening. Our ancient spiritual leaders, who were more like shamans, began to understand that the plagues were created by darkness bursting forth from the closet door. We had to go through a deep period of inner work that included embracing our shadows in order to heal ourselves.

Comparing your people to the ancient Pleiadians, you are not as frightened of the dark as we were. You are still a bit afraid, but that is normal. The repressed shadow energy on Earth is starting to burst out of the closet. Because you are all fractals, that means you feel it in your own way. It is just energy. Do not give it power or personify it by calling the shadow evil. It is just energy that has been ignored. It is energy of resistance and fear. You can release it without a story. Stories can end up distracting you and further empowering the shadow. Just allow the energy to flow out in the same way you would allow any energy to flow — little by little.

People have the temptation to dive into stories and blame the other side for every problem. That kind of consciousness only exacerbates polarity. Many people become activists, thinking they can change the world to their point of view. There is nothing wrong with serving your world, but activists have to be really conscious of their motivations. Are they marching for women's rights because it fills them with joy or because they are angry at the patriarchy? One has a different energy than the other. The energy that returns to you will be a reflection of your inner motivation and emotion. This is simple energy dynamics.

As the ego-suit becomes tighter and opposing sides get more polarized, you are given a challenge. What actions do you take, and are they in integrity? Are they based on deeper, still-unrecognized pain? These dilemmas are a reflection of the fractalized energy within you that still seek to be healed. There is no shame in this because all people experience the same challenge even if they don't speak about it or are not consciously aware of the pain they carry inside.

It might sound strange, but from our point of view as nonhumans looking at your reality, this is one of those special times on Earth that you will look back on with nostalgia and fondness. "Oh, look at those ancient humans — how hard third density was for them!" When you go through a challenging situation that you eventually conquer, you sometimes look back on that period of your life with fondness. Your future selves look back on this time with fondness. You make it through as a species because of the work you are doing now.

The resistance you see around you is because those shadow aspects don't want to change. They have a death grip on their view of reality. You can see that death grip as a sign of progress. In a polarized reality, one side acts with the same force as the other. Right now the loudest voice is the drama. You are not seeing the counterforce on the other side fueling the death grip by those who refuse change. That counterforce is your awakening consciousness, and this is what terrifies the opposite aspects within you that want to stay in control of reality. We are speaking both on the microcosmic (individual) level and the macrocosmic (collective) level.

Death and the Golden Lake

If we are each a piece of this hologram, what happens when we die? Do we go back into the bigger circle on the diagram?

This brings us back to the Pleiadian teachings of the Golden Lake. The Golden Lake can be equated with the hologram. The holographic energy is like golden plasmic liquid light. Using this model, you are a drop of the Lake. When you die, that drop returns to the Lake. This might be a radical model for some of you, because your spiritual teachings have been structured in a very linear way in terms of understanding past lives.

All of you are the Lake in your natural state, but you have had "separate" experiences. Using the metaphor, drops leave the Lake and move into separation. Each drop wears a little person-suit and goes about the business of living individually, and then the person-suit dies. The drop, named Jim as a human, goes back to the Lake. But it goes without the person-suit. The watery nature of the drop, much like a crystal, contains the experience the person-suit had. When it returns to the Lake, it dissolves like food coloring and goes into the whole body of the Lake. The Lake, being a hologram, contains all memory.

Then another drop emerges from the Lake. The previous person-suit that was named Jim already dissolved into the Lake, so you cannot say that this is a literal reincarnation. It is a brand-new, fresh drop that contains the holographic memory of Jim and every other drop that had a separate experience. When this drop emerges, it might carry with it some "Jim-ness." If this drop explores spirituality in its physical life, it might have a memory of being a guy named Jim in twenty-first-century Earth. The human ego will claim that memory as its own: This is "my" past life. But that memory belongs to the Lake, not to Jim or any singular being. This is why it seems more than one person can have a memory of the same life. Those memories belong to no one but the Lake. It has been very hard for the human ego to understand this, but it is getting easier. This is holographic consciousness, and it represents a foundation of our Pleiadian philosophy.

You are like an actor wearing a costume on a stage. The idea of waking up has to do with remembering you are on the stage in a costume playing a role. Don't forget this truth and think you are the character of Hamlet. Waking up is remembering you are not Hamlet. It is much more than a mental process. It is a visceral awakening that happens when you are ready.

The awakening process continues when you step off the stage. You are still aware of yourself in a person-suit, but you clearly see the drama is on the stage. You begin to detach from it. You become more of an observer of the drama rather than the one perpetuating it. You are no longer the performer. Awakening continues when you leave the theater altogether and have very little interest in the drama on the stage. These are the successive stages of awakening.

Returning to the distraught student's question earlier, she mentioned her disgust at all the people around her who are invested in conspiracy theories. Many believe that awakening means understanding who runs the show on Earth. This is very far from the truth and not what awakening means. Seeing control dramas on Earth as being layers of "truth" just means you are still on the stage, confusing your character with true reality. You cannot see anything clearly until you step off the stage.

Once you step off the stage, the view of reality is very different and does not contain the experience of polarization. Only the characters on the stage experience that intensity. As you step farther and farther away from the stage, the sun — the light of your consciousness — ignites and gets brighter, illuminating the characters on the stage for what they truly are.

You Must Do the Work to See Clearly

Many of you also have the temptation to cling to the so-called heroes in the stage play. In your time, there are many who claim to have inside knowledge of the play, and they attempt to weave an airtight view of reality that keeps their followers trapped and hooked on the daily drama, all the while thinking they are the only ones who know the truth and are free. There are no heroes in that way. Heroes don't create a narrative and feed it to you bit by bit in the insidious disguise of truth. These "heroes" are the ones who wish to control the stage play and keep you from exiting the stage. True heroes show you how to exit the stage rather than empower the drama. But when consciousness is polarized, it is very difficult to see those trying to control the narrative.

Often what these heroes rail against is actually the path to freedom. It is a paradox, indeed. Both sides believe only they can see clearly, but each side is deluded as long as it is polarized. This is what happens in the mirror house called Earth. Every reflection you see outside of you is distorted. Therefore, you can only look within *if* you have done the inner work needed to see clearly. If you haven't, then even the inner world is distorted.

Some mistakenly assume that exiting the stage means you should have no more use for the world, and you should become a hermit in a cave. This is not so. The paradox is that as you recognize all of this, you become more fully human. This is one of the paths of awakening the Sirians took. They finally embraced their bodies and the experience of being physical with no story. They felt their emotions without pushing them away. They could watch dramas unfold on the stage and not get sucked into them, because they were no longer afraid of their shadows. They could be fully present. This is what is meant by the phrase, "Be *in* the world but not *of* the world." This is not a dissociated state. It is actually a state of intense presence.

When the body dissolves, does the ego go with it?

The general answer is yes. As you know, the ego is basically an anchor. Its main function is to keep you grounded in physical reality. Your natural state isn't to be squeezed in a person-suit in a state of separation. When the body dissolves and your consciousness returns to the Lake, the anchor is no longer needed.

You can say the ego is like a recording device. It isn't that simplistic, but it is a good metaphor. When you return to the Lake, all the feelings, thoughts, and experiences that were distorted through the lens of the ego get transmitted into the Lake. Another drop might later emerge from the Lake carrying those same or similar distortions, and that drop continues the process of healing and awakening. That is how you might see patterns repeat over the span of many seemingly separate lives, but it isn't personalized. The patterns become unresolved imprints in the Lake that later crystallize in a drop that goes off to have an experience of separation in order to harmonize the discordant patterns. We are challenged by explaining this nonlinear concept in a linear framework. No patterns are "yours." They ultimately belong to the Golden Lake.

So the next questions might be: How do those patterns neutralize? At what point are unfinished patterns no longer repeated in the drops? In other words, when does healing happen?

To answer those questions, we have to return to the Sirian and Pleiadian teachings of the emotional-feeling body. As you are now, your Galactic Family were terrified of fully incarnating and truly feeling what it was like to be a physical being. Humans are far more sensitive than you have come to understand. You have the capacity to feel everything in a very refined way and without intense pain. It is only when you repress your natural ability to feel that your experience becomes even more painful. It is a paradox, yes?

This is where our Sirian and Pleiadian civilizations link to yours — the fear of feeling physical, mental, or emotional pain. We've already spoken about how ancient Pleiadians created a plague when they suppressed the darkness within them. The ancient Sirians also had to learn to work with the shadow in order to awaken themselves. All physical beings must embrace their true natures eventually. You must do the work to realize that many of your chronic conditions, such as migraines, immune disorders, back pain, and so on, are physicalized expressions of unrecognized emotional pain. When you address the emotional pain, the physical pain diminishes.

So how do you address emotional pain, especially if you aren't aware what the pain is? Physical pain exists for a reason: It asks you to pay attention. Sitting with your physical pain and meditating, contemplating, and journaling can miraculously reveal what lies beneath it, and it is always emotional pain from a distorted mirror reflection. The emotional pain might not be rational to your mind, but it affects you profoundly. There is a point where you can no longer deny it or it could literally destroy you.

Going back to the Golden Lake, those unfinished patterns neutralize when you stop denying them. When you embrace them, they no longer need to be repeated, and that particular wave pattern in the Lake becomes still.

To put it in linear terms, your entire journey — as the Lake and as the drop — leads back to stillness. That stillness is the state of rest, or the natural state of the One consciousness beyond duality. It isn't "out there." You already are that still Golden Lake. Only the fractals express the discordant patterns that seek to harmonize with the frequency of the Lake, and even they naturally gravitate toward harmony. Discordant energy often seems louder than stillness, which is why many of you only feel your stillness as a whisper.

Be Present

What is the key to navigating this journey? Allow yourself to relax into your awareness as a vast consciousness, like a golden lake. This lake has tides that match the in-breath and the out-breath of the universe. Let yourself be fully present with whatever you experience in any moment to the best of your ability.

Love and honor your unique golden drop as a part of the Lake, but know that the singular drop is fleeting. Only the Golden Lake is eternal. It is your true nature and your one Home.

About the Author

Lyssa Royal-Holt is best known for her groundbreaking books *The Prism of Lyra*, *Visitors from Within*, *Preparing for Contact*, and the first-of-their-kind *Galactic Heritage Cards*. She has been a channel, seminar leader, and contact researcher active around the world since 1985.

Lyssa's work is cutting-edge, and it is unique in that despite tackling otherworldly topics, her information is presented in a clear, concise, and grounded style. Her work has been translated into numerous languages worldwide and is considered to be included among the world's top channeled material.

Lyssa travels to Japan multiple times per year and regularly offers events in both Japan and the U.S.A. (Arizona). Currently, she can be seen in multiple episodes of the docuseries *Interview with E.D.* (Extradimensionals) on Gaia TV. For more information, please see her website, LyssaRoyal.net.

Galactic Heritage Cards

The overall concept of the *Galactic Heritage Cards* is to explore the journey from unity to fragmentation/polarity and back to reintegration. Since we all are part of one consciousness, this holographic journey unifies us all. The holographic concept proposes we experience unity and separation simultaneously. The components of the cards explore this journey in a variety of ways:

SPECIES OR STAR SYSTEM: The cards feature twenty-one species or star systems to symbolize the main archetypal groups who have influenced the development of our galactic family.

TIME STREAM OR "SUIT": Four suits, or time streams, are recognized — past, present, future, and parallel. They do not imply time in a rigid way but refer to the era of evolution from which the energy of each card is derived.

USING THE CARDS & GETTING STARTED: Each card has a theme or lesson connected to the civilization it depicts. Contemplative text and deeper commentary for each card are included in the booklet to help users understand how to apply this wisdom in their current lives, including several spreads to get you started.

ARTWORK: The architect of these cards, the multidimensional consciousness Germane (channeled through Lyssa), also assisted Hong Kong artist David Cow to channel the images. Contemplating the artwork of each card allows more information and energy to be transmitted, going beyond the commentary. The art connects deeply with the subconscious and adds a powerful dimension to the user's experience. The individual card art is also connected by an underlying image that represents our journey back to integration. It spans all the cards when they're laid out in a grid of 18 cards per row. Thus, the separate journey of each card carries an embedded energy of unity. The cards total 108 — a sacred number in many traditions that reflects the idea of wholeness and completion.

NEW EDITION
Full-color cards
are smaller &
easier to use

These cards are beautiful depictions of the different star lineages and their different challenges, strengths, and messages. These cards provide another layer of insights into this physical journey we are all having. They are absolutely right on and extremely insightful. Lyssa's work is truly, truly amazing! — J. P.

BY LYSSA ROYAL-HOLT & KEITH PRIEST

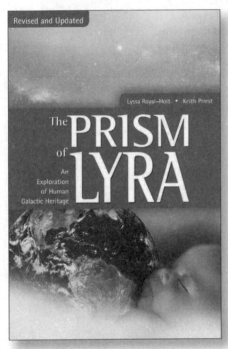

Revised and Updated

Lyssa Royal-Holt • Keith Priest

The **PRISM** of **LYRA**

An Exploration of Human Galactic Heritage

THE PRISM OF LYRA

AN EXPLORATION OF HUMAN GALACTIC HERITAGE

This is an introductory book that examines the idea of creation in a different light. In contrast to the notion that humans are the result of creation, it explores the idea that the collective humanoid consciousness (or soul) created our universe for specific purposes.

What are those purposes? Who is involved? These questions and many more are addressed, resulting in startling possibilities.

The Prism of Lyra then traces various developing extraterrestrial races (such as those from the Pleiades, Sirius, and Orion) through their own evolution and ties them into the developing Earth. Highlighted is the realization of our galactic interconnectedness and our shared desire to return Home.

Chapters Include

- Dimensional Infusion
- Creation of the Galactic Family
- The Womb of Lyra
- The Sirius Factor
- The Winds of Orion
- Earth's Pleiadian Cousins
- The Gateway of Arcturus
- Earth Inception
- Zeta Reticuli:
  Transformation and Awakening
- Integration: Coming Home
  to Ourselves

$16.95 • Softcover • 6 x 9 • 176 PP.
ISBN 978-1-891824-87-6

"[This] research on the stellar teachings (the meaning of the forms of knowledge from various star sources) is very accurate, complete, and meaningful. As we move into our time of merging (the time we have anticipated from the beginning of time when we would know our stellar brothers and sisters), [this] information about their essence is the truth."

— Barbara Hand Clow, author

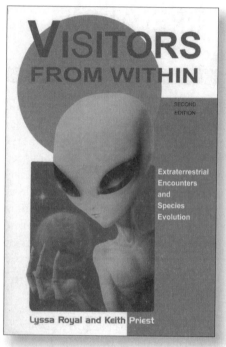

THROUGH ROBERT SHAPIRO

PHONE CALLS FROM THE FUTURE

Future History & Ancient History
from the People Who Were There

Explorer Race Book 27

The channel, Robert Shapiro, and the questioner live in different cities, so the channeling sessions are conducted over the telephone.

All the beings speaking through Robert in this book live now in the future in various times and places but have had lives on Earth or visited Earth during the times they speak about for this book.

$25.00 • Softcover • 320 PP.
978-1-62233-096-6

PART ONE: FUTURE HISTORY

- Mining on the Moon
- Life on the Moon
- Future from the Moon
- Doc's Identity
- Life on the Moon
- Water on the Moon
- The Origins of the Moon
- Stop Digging Toxic Matter on Earth and Live 700 Years
- Children and Dogs on Mars

PART ONE: ANCIENT HISTORY

- Spirits of the Biloba Tree Created Yeti (Bigfoot) People
- Protection from Earth's Violence
- Earth's History of ET Visitations
- Ancient Cultures Moved Stones through Love
- Gobekli Tepe, Turkey — Ancient Pleiadian Healing and Manifestation Circles
- Dolmens: ET Gifts to Ensure Early Humans' Survival

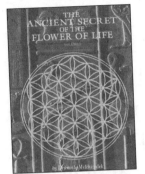

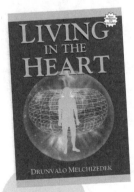